As the mother of an autistic son l[illegible]
relate to many of Kalisha and C[illegible]
remember meeting Kalisha for tl[illegible] years ago and
feeling so envious because she was so high-functional compared to my son. After reading this book, I now realize they had their own "crosses to bear" because she didn't really fit in with the "normal" kids, nor did she fit in with the true "handicapped" kids either. My heart breaks for all families who deal with this epidemic called autism. We're all just trying to raise our kids the best we can!

—LKS, parent

Gloria, I read your book yesterday. Loved it... I would love to pass this out to some of my parents and to new parents who are just starting on their journey with children of disabilities. Because no matter who we are, we all get down about ourselves in our roles as people, parents, mothers, fathers, friends, etc. and need to know that we are "not the only ones" living this life. There are tons of books out there explaining the medical where-tos and what-nots, but not too many with the comic/funny side of everyday living with someone with disabilities. I know I would prefer after knowing all the medical terms to read a book like this to know what my "real everyday life" was going to be possibly facing. This is a great job Gloria. Kudos to you!

—Jaime Buekers Schacher,
Special Needs Paraprofessional at
Homestead High School, Fort Wayne, IN

"Not Different Enough" brings you on an authentic journey, narrated by a mom who shares gut honesty in dealing with parenting a child with special needs. Gloria captures the array of emotion every parent encounters who is facing "disability" in their child, while amusing and validating her audience. From the uncertainty and fear of realizing "something is not okay with my baby" to the gut-honest "no-filter" moments that keep us fueled with laughter, to those monumental moments in which we celebrate victories most parents take for granted, to the painful moments of disappointment and acceptance of reality. Parents will identify and find comfort on every page.

As a parent of a child with special needs and multiple disabilities, I was able to identify with so many of the stages and stories of this dedicated, genuine mom. "Not Different Enough" validates the heart and soul of every parent dealing with a situation that no parent ever dreams of encountering. It envelops us with comfort, strengthens us with laughter, supports us with honesty, and challenges us with hope and faith! "Not Different Enough" brings me home in the most genuine way!

—Dina Diana, R.N.
parent of a child with multiple disabilities

Not Different Enough

A thirty-year journey with autism, Asperger's, and intellectual disabilities

GLORIA DOTY

Also by Gloria Doty:

An Ordinary Love Affair, included in an anthology titled: My Love to You Always

Devotions included in a 2014 devotional book titled: Penned from the Heart

Feeling Better, a first place short story included in the anthology: Flash of Fiction

Articles published in various magazines

Regular contributor to:

Hope-Full Living

daily devotions for Christian seniors

Ruby for Women—online magazine

a voice for every Christian woman

This book is dedicated to my daughter, Kalisha, with all my love.

You have taught me more about loving, forgiving
and accepting than I have taught you.

Contents

Epigraph

When I am afraid, I will trust in you. In God, whose
word I praise, in God I trust; I will not be afraid.
Psalm 56: 3-4 NIV

"Challenges are what make life interesting and
overcoming them is what makes life meaningful."
Joshua J. Marine

Sometimes the things we can't change end up changing us instead.
Unknown

Foreword

Dr. Cathy Pratt, BCBA-D
Indiana Resource Center for Autism

Thirty years ago, Gloria Doty gave birth to an amazing young woman, Kalisha. Diagnosed with various challenges including an Autism Spectrum Disorder, Gloria began a journey with her daughter to help her achieve all that was possible. Early on, institutionalization was suggested as it was for many of that age and generation. Gloria refused to accept that destiny and worked to find professionals who would support her dream for her daughter while treating them both with dignity and respect. This book highlights the triumphs and challenges. Gloria is amazingly honest about the mistakes she has made and about her decisions at various times. What is most striking to me is the conversation about guardianship, and how to balance keeping your child safe while allowing them to experience life. Taking these reasonable risks (and sometimes unreasonable risks), challenge every parent I know. As a result, Kalisha has made friends and had some amazing opportunities. And as a result, she has been a victim and suffered at the hands of criminals. Through it all, Gloria and Kalisha have maintained their faith. Toward the end, Gloria talks about preparing Kalisha for the time when Gloria dies. She candidly discusses her fears and her dreams, as well as Kalisha's.

Some things have changed since Kalisha was born. There is more awareness and understanding, and hopefully better service options. However, what have not changed are the tough issues that families must address. Gloria expresses some regret. After reading this book, I hope that Gloria will also celebrate the woman that Kalisha has become.

Preface

My purpose in writing this book is *not* to give clinical or medical advice. It is simply to give parents of young children on the spectrum, a look at long-term life and for all parents, a bit of hope and humor.

I chose the title "Not Different Enough" when Kalisha came home from school and told me, "Mom, the kids are mean to me. They don't know I have autism or anything, they just think I'm weird. I guess I'm not different enough." The title is not to imply I wish she had *more difficulties*. Every person with special needs has their own type of challenges.

As you read about our journey together, I pray you will have some great laughs, shed a few tears and perhaps nod your head when you recognize yourself or a family member in a similar situation or anecdote.

My daughter, Kalisha, will soon be thirty years old. She is a young woman with autism, Asperger's Syndrome and intellectual disabilities. These diagnoses were not all made at the same time in her life. The definition of the word "enigma" is: *somebody that is not easily explained or understood; a mystery.* That is truly descriptive of Kalisha. She is a female, and therefore, in the minority on the autism spectrum, as it affects many more males than females. She is extremely social and outgoing; not a usual trait of a person with autism.

Some of the difficulties we encountered could possibly have been avoided if I had had more information available to me when she was born in 1984. Although that seems fairly recent, there were no home computers, I could not Google my questions and I knew no one with an autistic child. Medical professionals were not much help at that time, either.

Things have definitely changed in thirty years as far as information is concerned and with 1 in every 88 children (some statistics from the CDC put the number as high as 1 in 50) being diagnosed with autism, there is a plethora of clinical information, therapies, food regimens and support groups available to parents and caregivers. As I talk to people, I find the missing information seems to be in descriptions of *everyday living* experiences. I have endeavored to give a glimpse into the failures, successes, trials and triumphs of Kalisha's life.

I have often been told I am a 'special parent.' That is simply not true. I am a parent with a *special* child/adult. I have made many mistakes, said and done the wrong things, banged my head against a wall and threatened to pack my bags and run for the hills. We live each day with faith and a sense of humor. Our adventures aren't over yet, I'm sure, but we have come this far and there is no turning back...for any of us.

All names, with the exception of Kalisha's siblings, have been changed, to protect the innocent *and* the guilty. Any mention of statutes, waivers and services are only as I know them in the state of Indiana. Please check the agencies in YOUR state of residence, as every state has different rules and regulations.

Acknowledgements

I want to acknowledge those who made this book possible. Lynnell Detraz, Janice Koenig, Kathy Sias-Head, Patti Simcoe, Carrie Sievers, Dawn Nichter and Amy Abbott for continually encouraging me in this endeavor. Jim Somers, Carla Logan and Marilyn Reinking for their willingness to read, re-read, make suggestions and push me to make it better. The people already named and many more who covered this entire project in prayer.

Thank you, Dr. Cathy Pratt, for agreeing to write the foreword and for giving me many pieces of wisdom and advice so many years ago. Thank you also, to the teachers and adults who befriended Kalisha throughout her life. You made a huge impact on her.

Thank you to my family who graciously pulled some facts from their memory banks and read various chapters to make certain the events were portrayed correctly. I especially want to thank Kalisha, who was willing to allow me to write all these chapters about her, without censoring any of the material.

Kalisha, 3-years-old, with her family at a wedding

Introduction:
You Don't Have To Attend

A very wise person gave me this advice several years ago. 'You do not have to attend every power struggle to which you are invited.' I was impressed. I'm sure I already knew that, but it was very liberating to hear someone say it.

It is such a simple but powerful concept. I have attended my share of power struggles with Kalisha. It is nearly impossible to explain the magnitude of her persistence; not just when she wants something but also when she wants you to see something from her viewpoint. It is not only hard work; it is exhausting.

I suppose stubborn, obstinate, unreasonable and bull-headed would all be descriptive; however, with Kalisha it is more than that. The autism comes into play and it is as though she has *blinders* on. Blinders are put on horses so they are not able to see to the side and be distracted. The horse can only look straight ahead. Kalisha can only focus on the *immediate*, not the future.

When she is in 'Kalisha Mode' as I call it, it is virtually impossible to reason with her. She refuses to see any dangers or consequences. She becomes a 'yabut.' That isn't from a foreign language; it is a word coined by a friend of mine. No matter what I say, Kalisha will counter with, "Yeah, but…"

The dentist used Novocain on her for the first time. Kalisha had never experienced a numb mouth before. The dental assistant warned her about trying to eat before the numbness wore off. It was dinnertime when we got home and she was hungry.

"I'll wait and eat with you later, Kalisha."

"Yeah, but I'm hungry now."

"I will make you a smoothie or some mashed potatoes."

"Yeah, but I can chew now."

"If you chew while it is numb, you will bite your cheek."

"Yeah, but if I move the food to the other side of my mouth, it will be okay."

"You won't be able to tell if it is on the other side or not."

"Yeah, but I can tell when it is on the left side."

At that point, I did what every wonderful exasperated mother of a yabut does; I said, "Fine, go ahead and eat. But if you bite your cheek and have blood running down your chin, I won't feel sorry for you."

Of course she didn't bite her cheek. Yeah, but……

An Institution...Really?

Kalisha was our fifth child; born 13 years after her siblings. No, she was not a 'mistake' as people often suggested. Her conception was actually planned. The surprise had been several years earlier, when at age 35, we learned we were going to be parents again. After the initial shock wore off, it was exciting. That pregnancy ended in a miscarriage; the first one I had ever experienced. I'm not certain if it was the grief of the miscarriage or the thought of a baby in the family again, but one or the other convinced us to try to get pregnant, intentionally.

The pregnancy itself was uneventful, as were all of my previous ones. It was an exciting time. It had been so long since there was a baby in the house; I no longer had any of the essentials. I still owned a crib and a high chair, but that was the extent of it. It was a good thing my friends had showers for me.

Things had definitely changed in 13 years. No pain relievers, no antacids, no cold medicines of any kind were allowed. Due to my *advanced* age of thirty-eight, I was advised to have an amniocentesis to determine any abnormalities in the fetus. I told my doctor there was no reason to have one because I would not abort the baby regardless of what the tests showed.

One thing *had not* changed: I had my babies *f-a-s-t.* This one was no exception.

I was barely settled in the labor room when I knew the birth was imminent. They wheeled me out into the hallway on the gurney, where a doctor I didn't know, was waiting for *her* patient to deliver. She quickly donned gloves and caught our baby.

Kalisha was in a hurry to get on with this thing called 'life' and life has not been the same since.

Kalisha did not seem to know how to nurse. She wanted to, she was hungry, but somehow she couldn't get her mouth placed in the right position. Even if she did, she couldn't create the suction necessary to stay latched on to the nipple. I tried every trick I had learned with my other 4 children, hoping I hadn't forgotten something vital in the last 13 years.

My mother came to visit and while changing Kalisha's diaper, she commented about the lack of fat on her little legs and buttocks.

"I think she's losing weight," Mom said. "She's not getting enough to eat."

That frightened me and I immediately started supplementing with formula from a bottle. She still didn't seem to have the ability to suck, at least not correctly. But she did get enough to sustain her and eventually, she seemed to be doing it right. Her lower jaw looked as though it was set too far back; almost as though she had no chin and her one eye would stray off to the side, especially when she was tired. I relayed all of this to her pediatrician, who didn't seem the least bit concerned. I reasoned if he wasn't worried about it, I shouldn't be, either. After all, he was the expert…right?

Kalisha grew and was alert, laughing and squealing, but never trying to form any words. She had no desire to get up on her knees and rock back and forth like my other children had done when wanting to learn to crawl. There seemed to be no strength or substance to her leg muscles. She did learn to roll over and eventually, she could sit up, unsupported.

When she was less than a year old, her sister, Kaylynn, was holding her when without any warning, Kalisha's eyes rolled back in her head and her body went totally limp. The EMS was called and transported her to the local hospital although she seemed perfectly fine by the time they arrived. All sorts of tests were conducted the next day.

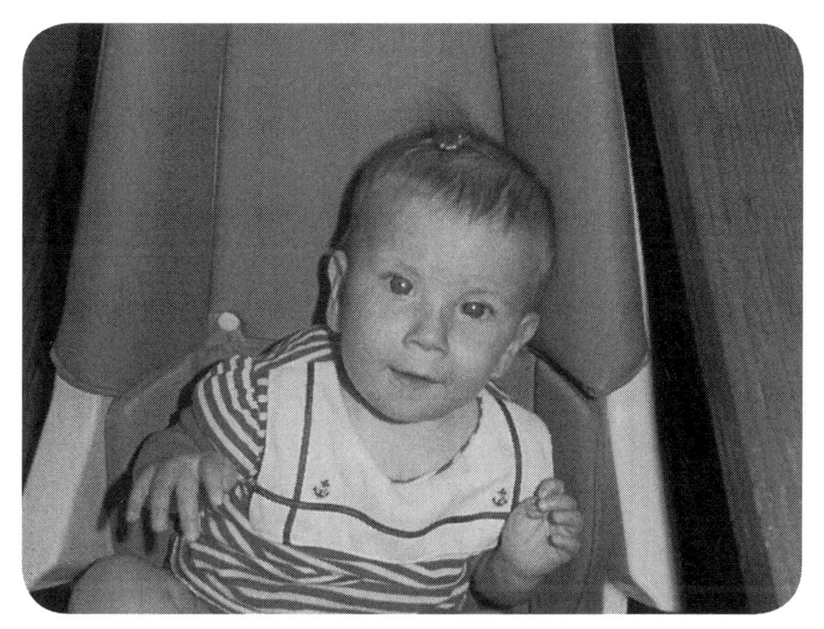

Kalisha at 6 months

None of the tests showed anything abnormal in brain activity, but they did show an abnormality in her blood. It was a Friday so we had to wait the entire weekend to hear the results. Because I had a sister who died of leukemia at age 2, I convinced myself that was what was wrong with Kalisha. I held her, rocked her, sang to her and prayed unceasingly for the 3 days. What a relief it was to hear the word mononucleosis. I was quite likely the only parent who ever *thanked* God when their child was diagnosed with mono. The doctor told me he had never had a patient that young who had it.

I believe I always knew in my heart there was something *not quite right* with Kalisha. I didn't want to admit it; you can live in denial for a long time.

At that time, there was a 15 minute segment on a local television station, detailing the activities and growth a child should be achieving at various ages. Kalisha could do none of the things they described. Although I continued to tell myself every child is different, they all accomplish things at different ages, I couldn't totally convince myself.

She was 18 months old. She did not say any words. She had learned to walk, but her balance was terrible and she spent more time falling down than walking.

It was time to find out what was going on. I approached her pediatrician and asked for some kind of tests (I had no idea what kind of tests: that was his job, right?).

He scheduled a battery of testing, during which I could not make one peep; just hold her on my lap. She accomplished some things correctly, but others didn't go so well. I didn't know how to feel when I left the building. Should I be happy she understood some of the instructions or sad about the tasks she couldn't accomplish? I was told to return in a few weeks to hear the results. Those were very long weeks, but the day finally arrived.

I sat in front of his desk, holding Kalisha on my lap.

"Your daughter is definitely behind in all areas. You need to contact an agency that deals with the handicapped."

His words hit me with the force of a tidal wave. A multitude of thoughts ran through my mind, but the lump in my throat prevented me from asking questions. Handicapped? Handicapped? How could he use that word to describe my baby? In my limited experience, handicapped meant blind, or in a wheelchair or totally incapacitated. Kalisha was none of those things.

I did manage to stammer, "What exactly does that mean?"

"Well, she will only fall farther and farther behind on every level as she gets older. You should start looking for an institution for her and get her admitted; the sooner, the better."

I picked Kalisha up, left his office and cried for the entire twenty-mile trip home. I simply could not wrap my mind around the doctor's words. I had grown up in a household where the experts were never questioned. As I drove, I talked to the Eternal Expert and prayed for his guidance. By the time I arrived, I knew I was not going to just blindly accept the verdict; I was not going down without a fight and I was definitely not going to put Kalisha in an institution.

I contacted an agency in our county and after being assessed and tested again, Kalisha was enrolled in a preschool for handicapped children (the term *special needs* was not in the country's vocabulary yet). I put our baby girl in a van three mornings a week. She was transported to school where she spent eight hours each day for those three days.

She received physical therapy, speech therapy plus sign language, gross motor skills therapy and a host of other helps. The physical therapist told me Kalisha should never have learned to walk. She said her center of balance was so far off, it should have been impossible. I was thankful for ignorance; we didn't know about her center of balance, so every time she fell down, we stood her back on her feet and finally, she gave up and walked.

I was as proud when she learned to step off a mat that was only 2 inches high as I had been when my other children learned to ride a bike. Success took on a totally different meaning with Kalisha.

Stop Re-Inventing the Wheel

KALISHA'S SCHOOL YEARS, all seventeen of them, were a long corridor, marked by many doors. Behind some of those doors were wonderful years with great teachers. Some doors held indifferent teachers, some, totally oblivious teachers and some hid hateful teachers. I wasn't always sure she would survive and most of the time, I was pretty certain *I* wasn't going to survive.

She started attending The Blue School, (as Kalisha called it because it was painted blue,) when she was 18 months old. A van picked her up 3 mornings a week and transported her to Columbia City, a town 10 miles away from our home in the country. She would stay there for the entire school day. It was one of the most difficult things I ever had to do; I would hand her over to the driver who carried her to the van, settled her in a seat and fastened her seatbelt. Although I smiled, was encouraging and would wave until they were out of sight, I would cry when I went back into the house. It didn't seem fair that she had to spend all day in school when she should have been able to be a toddler and have fun at home, but sometimes nothing seemed fair for her.

The Blue School was actually a fantastic experience for Kalisha. She learned so much she never would have learned at home. It was a preschool for children with various handicaps, run by an agency that served adult handicapped clients, in our county. Kalisha received physical therapy, speech therapy which incorporated sign language until she learned to talk, and occupational therapy. The person in charge of this magical place was Pam Watson. She was an angel in human form; seriously. Pam knew more about Kalisha and all the other children who attended there and their behaviors than anyone I had known before or have known since.

Kalisha blossomed. She loved it there. She was even chosen to be on the front of the county's United Way brochure. She learned many things besides talking and walking. She learned to share, to compromise, to listen to the people in charge, and to pretend, a little. Although pretending was, and still is, difficult for her, she tried.

'Pretending' in the kitchen at The Blue School

She had friends there. She wanted to be like them. She wanted to BE them. There was an incident in a McDonald's lobby that I can see like it was yesterday. While standing in line and scanning the menu board, I heard a child squalling and screaming. I turned to look, as did everyone else in the crowded lobby. I wondered why the parent didn't come get the little girl who was causing all the commotion by lying on the floor and kicking her feet. Wait..it was Kalisha. I briefly considered leaving her on the floor and pretending I didn't know her, but I didn't. I stood her on her feet and asked why she was doing that.

"Jenny does it all the time," she told me.

Jenny was one of her classmates and she did have meltdowns like that. It was difficult for Kalisha to understand why Jenny could behave that way but she couldn't. Kalisha still labors under the *'if she can do it, why can't I?'* train of thought and it's almost thirty years later.

She was given a scholarship to attend a church preschool for *typical* children, one day a week. This preschool had 2 awesome, loving, Christian women in charge. They had been 'briefed' by Pam about what strategies worked with Kalisha and what didn't. They went out of their way to help Kalisha with the things she struggled with but the other children her age could do; something as small as opening a wrapper on a snack.

When Kalisha was 5-years-old, she had to attend 'regular' kindergarten. Her diagnosis was changed from 'developmentally delayed' to 'mildly mentally handicapped' or MIMH. The public school system did not recognize the developmentally delayed label, so it was necessary to change it. I suggested the kindergarten teacher meet with Pam to acquaint herself with some of Kalisha's traits and peculiarities. She declined. Then I offered to buy coffee if she would please meet with Pam. She adamantly refused; saying she knew what she was doing and didn't need any input.

This type of thinking became a pattern for several years in school. They wasted so much time reinventing the wheel each year. The new teacher would always refuse to glean any information from the teacher of the previous year. The result was at least the first 3 months of every school year were wasted while the new teacher tried to figure out how to handle some of Kalisha's behaviors. It was ludicrous. They were all so insecure; they didn't want to admit they might learn something from someone else. Unfortunately, it was the children who suffered.

Kindergarten and first grade were spent at a school in Columbia City, 10 miles away. This meant she had to ride the regular school bus for an hour in the morning and an hour in the afternoon. The worst part was she had to ride the *high school* bus. She was the only 'child' on it. A few months before school started that year, I saw the bus driver, whom I had known for years.

I teasingly told him, "I hear you're going to take my little girl to school this year."

"Yeah, and I wish to h_ _ _ I didn't have to."

Wow. I was not prepared for that. I told myself he didn't know what Kalisha might do and that made him afraid. Fear often turns into anger.

For the most part, her long bus rides were uneventful. She sat in the seat immediately behind the driver and although he wasn't happy about taking her, I knew he would not let anything happen to her. Kalisha; however, soon won his heart. As a Christmas gift, he gave her a replica yellow metal school bus and a Rudolph puppet. She still has them both.

Long rides on the school bus.

She did learn a few colorful words while riding with teens. There was a day when she announced she had to go to the principal's office that day. Curious, I asked why. She answered, "Well, I said f____, and the teacher didn't like that word." I'll bet she didn't.

I did explain it wasn't an appropriate word to use; however, I thought, to myself, she had done pretty well by not saying it until she had been riding with all those teenagers for several months.

As second grade approached, it was decided she would attend an elementary school that was only a mile from our house. It was a relief to know she wouldn't have that long bus ride anymore.

Once again, no teacher would talk to the teacher from the previous year. It was frustrating. When she misbehaved in class, no one knew what to do. I gave suggestions: a picture list taped to the top of her desk because she worked better with visuals, a time alone to 'de-stress' when she became too stimulated.

The school's solution was to have a 'booth' built and if she wouldn't stay in her seat or talked all the time, she had to go to the booth and complete her work. It looked somewhat like a telephone booth with clear sides, so she could see. It was placed in the hallway outside the office. It seems rather barbaric now, but this was 23 years ago and I still labored under the assumption that schools knew what to do.

During her third grade year, I insisted she be tested for autism. I knew very little about autism; only the things I had read or heard, but I had been observing some of those behaviors in Kalisha since she was quite young. When she was 6-years-old, I made an appointment with a professor at a local college. She had the reputation of being the 'autism professional' or 'autism god' as I called her. She was said to know everything there was to know about autism. She took Kalisha to her office and returned within 10 minutes.

"She definitely does not have autism. She's too verbal."

I didn't accept her verdict, even if she was the expert. I observed entirely too many behaviors to believe her. I started keeping a written record of behaviors. After several years in the school system, I knew she needed a 'label' if she was ever going to receive any help. I contacted the Indiana Resource Center for Autism at Indiana University. The Director and I talked many times. She arranged for a team to come to Kalisha's school and do an assessment.

After their visit, the consensus was Kalisha indeed was autistic and now we had a piece of paper to prove it.

I learned all sorts of new words and terminology. *Inclusion* and *least restrictive environment* and *IEP* (Individualized Education Plan) were a few of them. Although inclusion was touted as the best thing since sliced bread, I was not a big fan. As usual, the state put the cart before the horse. It was mandated every special needs child was to be included in the regular classroom; however, there had been no preparation of the teachers for this. How were they supposed to instruct the other children if they had to spend a large portion of their day with the special needs children? It was a lose-lose situation, in my opinion. I understood the premise that the typical children would learn to accept the ones who were different and the world would be wonderful. Unfortunately, it doesn't always work that way. I also didn't believe children like Kalisha should be locked away in a Special Education room and never be with their peers, but total inclusion was a disaster until it was decided Kalisha qualified for an aide. The aide helped with academic and social situations.

This was also my first experience with the IEP. The requirements to dot every 'i' and cross every 't' are so stringent, it takes an inordinate amount of time to complete one and in the end, you have a stack of papers at least one inch thick. Every page must be completed in triplicate. I have a very large storage tub, filled with Kalisha's IEP papers. The IEP is a necessary evil but can be very helpful. Each subject and class is outlined and attainable goals are listed. If the plan is not followed by the teacher, a parent has recourse to make certain it is done correctly. The first one we attended lasted over 4 hours.

It was fourth grade before there were 2 teachers who were honestly interested in learning from the previous teacher. Thank you, Lord. These two women made Kalisha's fourth grade her very best year in school… ever. They taught her, accepted her, laughed with her and totally 'got it.'

An example: Mrs. B. came to school with her hair a different color than normal. *No Tact Kalisha* said, "Mrs. B. Your hair is purple. Ooh, I don't like it." Instead of getting defensive or having her feelings hurt, Mrs.

B. told Kalisha, "Yes, I know. My husband isn't wild about it either." Then they had a good laugh about her purple hair. The other teacher, Mrs. O., taught her to tie her shoes (a difficult task for a person with almost non-existent small motor skills) and worked diligently with her on her reading and comprehension. Kalisha could read fairly well by the end of the year, but math continued to be a struggle for her.

Fifth grade was another good year. Kalisha had an aide with her for the entire day. She adored the aide, a young woman who genuinely seemed to like Kalisha, wanted her to be accepted and to learn as much as she could.

Next stop: junior high. New building, new classmates, new aide, new routines…

Junior High...and Low

Junior High was a whole new ballgame; a new building, new routine, new schedules and new classmates. All those new experiences were scary for Kalisha. She continued to have an aide with her, but of course, the aide was new and unfamiliar, also.

This was her first experience with multiple classrooms and going from one to another all day. She had a math teacher with whom she immediately bonded. This young woman helped Kalisha understand some basic math concepts.

Junior High consisted of some very high *highs* and some really low *lows*. One of the highs was when she decided she wanted to try out for cheerleading. I tried to discourage her in the beginning because I didn't want her to be hurt or humiliated. The coordination needed for cheerleading was not one of Kalisha's strengths.

She wanted to try so badly, I reluctantly gave my permission. She went to every practice, then came home and told me what was required. She couldn't do half the things on the list, but she wanted to continue. Tryouts were on a Saturday. She chose to wear the T-shirt that had Rudy Reuttiger's autograph on it.

We had attended a conference where Rudy was the speaker. She purchased a shirt with his mottos on it and had him sign it. She also watched the movie of his life several times. I said lots of prayers during the tryouts; not that she would be chosen, but that she would do her best. They were not open tryouts so I couldn't stay and watch.

When I picked her up, she was grinning from ear to ear.

"I made it," she said as she climbed into the car.

Being such a good mother, I said, "You're kidding! How in the world did you make the squad?"

She continued to smile and said, "Well, I did just like Rudy. I prayed and then I did my best."

The cheerleading coach was responsible for her being included by the other girls. They allowed her to set on the floor in front of their pyramids, and join in when she could do the movements.

Kalisha, center back, with the cheerleading squad

She also wanted to join the track team. The track coach allowed her to run one of the shorter races, but she only competed in the first 2 meets. There were several reasons for her wanting to quit. 1) She didn't like finishing last and 2) She said it hurt her breasts too much to run. (Yes, she did have a sports bra, but she was also very well endowed)

P.E. was not a good class. Instead of allowing her to do some exercises that she was able to do, she was always expected to compete with the rest of the class. Most of the activities were beyond her motor skill capabilities.

She hated the required showers; the undressing in front of all the other girls. I don't believe there is any junior high girl who likes the shower room, but as you can imagine, the remarks made to her were unusually cruel. One of the particularly nasty girls became very angry with Kalisha in the locker room. She kicked her in the shins; hard enough to leave bruises. Then she grabbed Kalisha's glasses off her face and threw them in the trash can. Kalisha is nearly blind without her glasses, so she was in panic mode for a few minutes until she found them. They were, of course, bent out of shape and barely stayed on her nose until she got home.

It was increasingly difficult to get her up in the morning and ready when the bus came. It was a daily struggle which often resulted in me having to drive her to school because she missed the bus. I informed her in no uncertain terms the next time she missed the bus due to not getting up and dressed, I was taking her to school in her pajamas. I learned early on not to make threats if you aren't prepared to carry them out, so you know the day came when I delivered her to school in her pajamas and slippers. I called ahead so they would know why she wasn't dressed. I knew she had shoes and some clothes in her gym locker, so I was pretty sure she would have something to wear.

She didn't miss the bus again. Was she embarrassed? Yes, I'm sure she was. Should I have done it? Probably not. The point is this: her perpetual defiance in the mornings and her tardiness had nothing to do with her disabilities. It was a question of her will pitted against mine. In this case, I won.

I'm not advocating you do the same. I am a firm believer in fitting the punishment or consequence to the crime and I had cajoled, wheedled, pleaded, insisted and explained enough. I also told you I would be honest about my mistakes.

In the middle of her last year of Jr. High, I couldn't stand the daily persecution of Kalisha. I made the decision to homeschool her. It was not a well thought-out plan. In fact it was a total knee-jerk reaction to several factors: I was tired. I didn't think I could fight one more IEP (individualized education plan) battle or one more stubborn teacher or think about her struggling to fit in with kids who had no desire to accept her. I had not done any research on homeschooling; I wasn't prepared, but I bull-headed my way through it.

I would not consider it one of my better decisions; at least not the way I handled it. At that time, there were not nearly the resources available for homeschooling as there are today. I didn't check for a curriculum or talk to other homeschooling parents. I was in survival mode and did exactly what Kalisha often does: don't think of future consequences or plans, just 'do it' and deal with the fall-out later. (Makes you question which one of us is autistic, doesn't it?)

A friend volunteered to help with science; I worked with her on simple math concepts and she read a 'billion' books from the library. I was fortunate I had a job where I was allowed to take her with me to work; not every day, but many days. I was the Director of Children's Ministries for a large church. My 'office' was in a very large kids' gathering room. She could work on homework, watch a movie, read, take a nap, or go for walks. It did not interfere with my work requirements. It was an ideal situation.

You know how children will usually listen to someone other than their parent when it comes to teaching. Kalisha was no exception. She didn't particularly like my method of teaching, she got tired of being with me at work all day and she truly missed the whole school setting.

I realized I could not continue homeschooling for the next 3 years of high school, so I re-enrolled her in the fall and prayed daily that she and the other students had matured enough for some things to be different. Not so.

High School...the Good, the Bad and the Ugly

HIGH SCHOOL WAS an interesting conglomeration of mountaintop experiences and unbelievably rock bottom situations. Occasionally, they happened on the same day, which could drive a mere mortal insane. I vacillated between wanting to buy flowers for some teachers and students and wishing others would fall off the face of the earth. In fact, I was willing to push some of them off.

Kalisha had to board the bus at a designated spot. Remember, we lived 10 miles from town; finding another bus stop was not an option. There was one particular girl at this bus stop who would shove Kalisha out of line EVERY morning, while calling her every nasty name she could think of. I spoke to the bus driver, but he didn't see it, so he couldn't do anything.

The same girl would knock Kalisha against the wall and call her a retarded b___ when they passed in the hallway. We went to the police station and tried to file a restraining order against her, but because the girls weren't related, it was impossible. This was before 'bullying' became an everyday word. It was, however, an everyday occurrence. The principal made a chart detailing the halls these 2 girls could use to get to classes, without ever having to pass each other. That worked, although Kalisha's route was quite circuitous, through the back halls. This occasionally caused her to be late for class, which got her in trouble, too. It was a no-win situation.

Kalisha was desperate for the other 'kids' to like her and would often do anything they suggested. This never had a good outcome. They would tell her, "See that kid in that classroom? He really likes you. Go in and kiss him." Sometimes she would do it. I'm sure you can imagine how that would turn out: teacher angry, boy embarrassed and angry; instigators loving it.

Or they would coax her into pinching some boy's backside as he walked past, telling her again, how much he liked her and would like it if she did that. It was a never-ending harassment, partly due to the fact she wanted them to like her. No matter how much I talked and explained their motives, she still believed they would be her friends if she did what they said.

There were some teachers who were worse than the students. During one IEP meeting, I stressed Kalisha's desire to be in an art class. I suggested the need for modifications, of course, but she could do some of the projects. The teacher refused to have her in her class. I reminded her of my *2-inch thick* book of parental rights and suggested she rethink her position. She adamantly refused to have Kalisha in her class, citing all the reasons it would be detrimental to her other students.

If you know me at all, you realize that was akin to waving a red flag in front of a bull. I did, however, acquiesce and agree to an alternative class. The *only* reason I did, was because I knew what hell Kalisha's life would be like with that ignorant woman for a teacher. I couldn't do that to Kalisha. I had all sorts of thoughts about what I wanted to do to the teacher, though.

Another class was photography. At the IEP, I suggested to this teacher that he give Kalisha a disposable camera instead of the 'big lens' 35 mm camera. All she needed was to learn how to center her subjects, make sure the light was right, etc. Oh, no. He insisted she would do just fine with the big camera and all the settings. Stupid man. She brought that camera home, put it on her dresser and never touched it again until she turned it in at the end of the semester.

This class also had a dark room for developing the students' pictures. The smells of the chemicals were offensive to Kalisha, so she never wanted to be in the dark room. During one class period, several senior boys in the class, (yes, I said SENIORS) coaxed her into entering the dark room, closed the door and held it shut while they told her, "We don't want no f_______ retards in our class." Thankfully, a girl in the class went to get the teacher. Did I complain? You know I did. Loud and long. Were the boys punished or suspended? No. Did I want to flatten their tires, pour sugar in their cars' gas tanks? Absolutely. Kalisha wanted to pray for them so they would have Jesus in their hearts.

Lest you think all her days were filled with horror, they were not. She joined the choir (she sings notoriously off-key). She even competed in a music competition, singing a solo. She had a Child Development class she totally enjoyed. Just like in the sit-coms, she brought a 'baby' home. This baby cried, needed fed, changed, all the bells and whistles. Kalisha did fairly well with it. She wasn't too excited about getting up in the middle of the night when it cried. We talked a lot about the word REALITY.

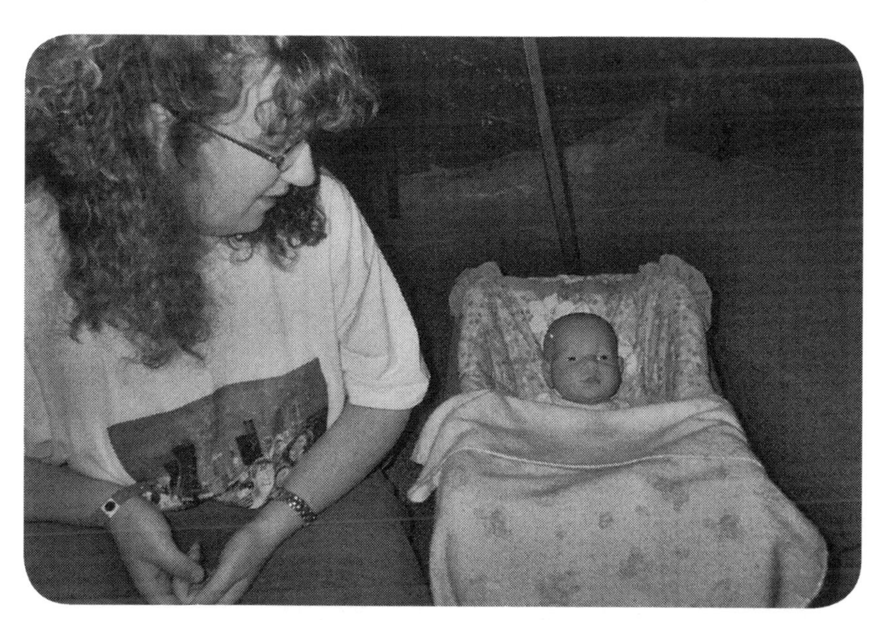

Child Development Class a dose of reality

She got to play on the girls' Powder Puff football team (they only play one game before Homecoming). She helped decorate for the Senior Prom. She had the opportunities for a few jobs during school hours. She made lots of acquaintances and some very good friends. Many of the students were wonderful. It only takes a handful to make life miserable. AND as the goal of school should always be...she learned academically, also. The courses were too difficult for her to grasp entire concepts but she managed to retain some knowledge and then build on that.

We moved from our home in the country to Fort Wayne the summer before her senior year. She wanted to graduate from *her* high school, so I drove her back and forth to school every day for the entire school year.

One of the mountain top experiences of her senior year was to attend the Senior Prom. When Kalisha was a freshman and attended the youth group at our church, many of the girls would talk about their excitement of going to the prom; dresses, hair, nails, flowers, etc. Kalisha would say, "I want to go to the prom one day."

A young man in Youth Group who was a few years older than Kalisha, told her to call him when she was a senior. He would take her to the prom. When that time rolled around, she remembered his promise and asked if I thought we could find him. I contacted someone who knew he was attending college in a neighboring state. I hesitated, but said a prayer for confidence and dialed the number. When I said hello, his first words were, "It must be time for Kalisha's prom. I've been waiting for this call." If it were possible to hug someone through a phone, I would have. His remembering of that long ago promise made me cry.

We made the arrangements, Kalisha bought the tickets and I sent him gas money. (It was a long trip and he was a college student.) Kalisha's sisters helped her with her hair, nails and a little make-up. Between *shopping* for a dress, having to *wear* a dress and dressy shoes, she was beginning to wonder if this was worth it. It was totally out of her comfort zone. Talking about it was one thing, actually doing it was another.

He showed up at the appointed time, with a corsage. We took pictures and I watched as he held the door open for her and helped her into his car. It was very emotional for me; not because she was going to the prom, but because it seemed like such a 'normal' event in her life when there weren't too many of those.

Kalisha and friend, Drew, at the Senior Prom

They had a great time; they danced (I would love to have witnessed that) they ate, they mingled and he brought her home, safe and sound. The next day, she was watching a kid's movie; like she was 11 years old instead of the grown up young woman who went to the prom the night before.

She remembers her high school years with mostly happy memories. Sometimes she will say, "I wish I could go back to high school." She has seen many of her classmates in various settings over the years; they always remember her. In fact, her current Case Manager attended the same high school as Kalisha which produced an instant bond.

I truly wish I had many do-overs for her years in school. It always seemed to be a balancing act of deciding what 'rights' I should enforce without harming Kalisha and her relationship with a teacher. There are many difficult decisions for parents but we do the best we can. Is it always the right decision? No.

When it was time for graduation, we did all the 'senior' things; had her pictures taken, ordered the invitations, bought the usual Class of 2003 shirts and jewelry and planned a party.

She did not receive a diploma because her grades were not high enough. The alternative to a diploma is a Certificate of Completion. It looks like a diploma, but of course, the words printed inside are different. At that time, these were issued to students who didn't meet the grade requirements but had attended classes.

She was thrilled to wear her cap and gown and cross the stage with her classmates. I could tell she was searching for her sisters and me on the bleachers. She found us and it was apparent she was smiling from ear to ear. We, however, were all crying.

Sisters, Kari, Kendra and Kaylynn with Kalisha at graduation

Goin' Through the Big 'D'... and I Don't Mean Dallas

In case you're not a country music aficionado; that's the title of a song. Divorce is definitely not something to laugh about or treat lightly, but that was the title that popped into my head when I decided to write a chapter about it.

I have often been asked if I thought having a special needs child was to blame for our divorce after nearly 40 years of marriage. Statistics do indicate the rate of divorce is extremely high in homes with individuals with special needs. There were many reasons for our marital problems. While I believe that Kalisha and her care was just one more thing for us to argue about, it was definitely not the sole cause of our separation and ultimate divorce.

I am not going to dredge up our many disagreements. I am only addressing the divorce in this book because it did involve Kalisha. Her feelings about it and her reactions to it might help other parents dealing with a divorce.

Kalisha's father was a truck driver and was gone for days at a time. Through no fault of his, he wasn't there for the everyday crises that arose. I made decisions without him. I had to, because many times the decisions could not wait. I was the one responsible for her transportation, appointments, school activities, medical emergencies and attending workshops. When he would be home, I believe I resented his 'intrusion' into our world. I didn't realize that at the time, but I do now.

The night I told him to leave there was a lot of verbal confrontation between us. We obviously woke Kalisha. She came down the stairs, took one look at the two of us and started to cry. He left; I held her and attempted to explain. I believe I said all the usual things: your dad loves you, he's angry with me, not you, and he will always be in your life. Although Kalisha rarely cried, she did cry that night. She never cried about it again.

When the decision was made that we separate, he moved to an apartment in a town 20 miles away. In the beginning, Kalisha's world, specifically, didn't really change. We were used to him not being there, so there was no difference. She was 12 years old at the time. We (her dad and I) carried the separation out entirely too long. Neither of us wanted to officially end the marriage. As long as we had a glimmer of hope of reconciliation, I suppose Kalisha did, too. Again, in retrospect, I believe it would have been better for all concerned and especially Kalisha, if we had made a decision and finalized it quickly. As I look back on that period in our lives, I realize I should have found a counselor for Kalisha and for me to help us work our way through this loss, but I didn't. I certainly prayed about our situation every day, which helped immensely and was the only way we survived.

He was supportive when I was seeking legal guardianship in court and when she needed help with recovering many, many of her DVDs that had been stolen by an acquaintance and I knew he would come to her defense in a heartbeat.

There was an occasion when I asked if Kalisha could stay with him for the weekend, as I had to go out of town. He said no because he and his wife were going to Michigan. When I told Kalisha, she said, "Why can't I go with them? It's not like he has to help me in the bathroom or anything." Good point. I wondered the same thing.

She does make some humorous statements some times. One day as we were talking, she said, "Do you think when Dad dies, anybody will call and let me know or will we just read it in the paper?" I assured her I thought someone would let her know.

I tried then and still try, not to speak badly about him, especially in front of Kalisha. Occasionally, she will make a statement about something which I'm sure she has overheard me say. Okay. Make SURE your child doesn't hear your remarks about their parent.

There are always the times when she gets really angry with me and yells, "I'm going to live with my dad. He would let me do "fill in the blank" That used to hurt my feelings, but now I just grab her overnight bag, hand it to her and tell her to start packing her things.

She and I both know she wouldn't last at his house for more than a few hours. He lives a totally different lifestyle than she is accustomed to and unless she is going to pack her laptop, her TV with her 200+ DVD collection, her bookcase full of books and about 50 pieces of Colts clothing, she won't be staying long.

Divorce is never easy, on anyone. I asked her before I wrote this if she remembered being sad, angry, or feeling abandoned. Her answer was, "No, but I did blame him for us having to move away from the farm."

Kalisha can carry on a grown-up conversation with nearly anyone. He could discuss a large variety of topics with her, but he doesn't. It is his loss because she has become a very interesting person.

Words, Books and Movies

KALISHA HAS ALWAYS loved pictures *and* words. When she was quite young, I would occasionally entertain her during a church service by getting out every photo in my wallet. She would scrutinize each one, endlessly. At home, she would take a package of newly developed pictures and spread them out on the floor, as if she were going to play Concentration.

She was careful with them, would crawl around the perimeter of her laid-out pictures and examine them for hours. Perhaps the pictures were the driving force behind her love of reading. She started by 'reading' picture books. She really didn't have an imagination but she knew enough words to be able to match them to the pictures on the pages.

She learned to read phonetically, starting in preschool. Once she could recognize the letters of the alphabet, she could sound them out. Kalisha had an extensive vocabulary. I attributed it to the fact she lived with parents and 4 siblings who all liked reading and words and used them in the correct context. If I used a word I thought she didn't know, I would backtrack and explain the definition. I still do that today. If I or someone else in the conversation makes a statement I'm not sure Kalisha understands, I will stop and ask her, "Do you know what that means?" Many times she does and can articulate the meaning, but sometimes, she will say she doesn't know. I explain right then while it is fresh in her mind.

When her nieces and nephews were very young, she would pretend to *read* to them every chance she got or when she convinced them to sit still long enough. Unfortunately for her, they all got older and learned to read better than she did, so she continued to read aloud, but for her own enjoyment.

Kalisha's love of books, reading and the library bordered on obsession at times. I dropped Kalisha and her niece, Elizabeth, at the library to pick out a few books. When I returned to pick them up, they were each struggling to balance a stack of books, literally higher than their heads.

I asked, "How many books do you have there, Kalisha?

"I don't remember. I think forty-five."

"Pick out 5 to take home and return the rest, right now. You cannot have 45 books checked out at once." In my head, I was asking, 'Doesn't the library have a limit on the number of books one person can check out?' Apparently not.

She has never lost her love of books or the library. She learned how to find and reserve books, online. On one occasion, when she was in her teens, I noticed that some of the books she was bringing home from the library had fluorescent pink labels attached to them. I asked what that meant. She told me they were national library loans. I listened while she explained. When the book she wanted was not available at any of the public library branches in our city, they had to get it from somewhere else in the country. I didn't even know that was possible.

The reason she HAD to have them is because she reads all of the books in a series, and could not go on with the series until she had the next book. She has read every Disney book, all of the Full House, Michelle, Boxcar Children, Goosebumps and Baby Sitter Club series.

There are 143 Baby Sitter Club books. After she finished all 143 from the library, she started a quest to *own* all of them. She searched E-Bay, the Half Price bookstore, Borders and Barnes and Noble. She didn't care if they were used; she just needed them all.

All her books have to be kept in numerical order on her bookshelves and they are returned to the shelves in the right order. After she finally got the entire set, she started reading them all over again from #1. Remember...she had just read all 143 from the library. If you have ever read a Baby Sitter Club book, you know that *every one* starts out with the telling of how the Baby Sitter Club got started. So, if it were you or me, we would skip that part and get to the story. Not Kalisha! She reads every word in every book. How do I know that? She reads out loud. (I can almost recite the beginning of the books) AND she has a reading ritual. Same times, every day. AND she reads 6 or more books at a time; one chapter in each book, until she has read a chapter in all 6. How does she remember what is going on in each book? I don't have a clue! That is most likely an Asperger's trait, but when she started that ritual, that diagnosis had not yet been made.

Reading a chapter in several books at one time.

If you happen to come into the room in the middle of her reading time, she will read to herself, but would rather you leave so she can read aloud again.

I am not certain how much she retains, but she can usually give an overview of the contents of a book. If you listen to her read (sometimes, it is impossible not to) you realize she reads fast and if she comes to a word she can't pronounce, she just picks out a few of the letters and makes a new word.

Example: She was reading aloud a list of ingredients for a recipe.

"2 cups of flour, 1 cup sugar, 2 eggs, ½ cup butter, vanilla ex-lax.."

"Whoa, wait a minute. What did you just say?" I asked.

She repeated, "Vanilla ex-lax"

"Kalisha, look at that word. Does it say *extract*?"

"Oh yeah, I guess it does."

While reading an article from the newspaper about the post office delivering mail to *clustered* mailboxes, she said, *cluttered* mailboxes. I had her read it 3 times and she said cluttered each time. I suppose she could understand cluttered mailboxes, but didn't think the word clustered could go with mailboxes.

While many neurotypical children love to read, Kalisha's autism gives her reading some unique traits. She not only reads what is inside the book, she doesn't consider the book finished unless she has read every word in it and *on* it; even the back cover. If it is part of a series, the words on each back cover are exactly like all the other back covers, but she has to read each one.

She has to finish a chapter to be able to put the book down. I am serious when I say, 'If there was a tornado warning, or a fire alarm blaring, it would take every fiber in her body to stop reading and move to a safe place, if she was not at the end of a chapter.'

She is just as ritualistic about her movies. DVDs come with a small brochure listing every scene in the movie. That is an essential piece for Kalisha. She pauses the movie before each scene while she reads the description of the next scene.

She purchased a used Cinderella movie but alas, when she got it home, the paper was not inside. She returned it and found another one that contained the scene paper. When she orders DVDs online or purchases them from e-Bay, she contacts the seller first and makes certain the movie contains the scene paper.

She has a system for watching every movie she owns. I asked how she knows which ones she has watched and which ones she has not watched. Does she write the titles down in a notebook to keep track of them? She told me she does not write them down, she *just knows.*

Kalisha has an extensive DVD collection of more than 200 movies. They are kept in a large black case, each in its own pocket. She owns a variety of titles. Some are quite childish while others are much more mature: Titanic, Forrest Gump, Twister, The Notebook, Mean Girls, etc. She also has DVDs of complete TV series, such as all 9 seasons of Little House on the Prairie.

Extensive DVD collection

Even though she pays for her movies and books with her own money, she is very generous with them. She takes 4 with her every week to cooking class where she gives them to one of her classmates. The classmate returns the 4 Kalisha loaned her the previous week. When a friend had an operation and was homebound, she asked Kalisha for movies. Kalisha loaned her the titles she requested. I plead with her to write down the titles she is loaning, but she says it isn't necessary. She knows which ones are loaned out.

I have no doubt she does.

Discipline..S

DISCIPLINE IS ALWAYS a contested topic, regardless of whether it is focused on neurotypical children or special needs children. I have 4 typical children and 1 special needs child, so I have seen the varying aspects of discipline with both groups of individuals; but this book is not about how or when I disciplined my other children; only Kalisha.

I did discipline her, sometimes unjustly, I am sure. I remember telling someone Kalisha received more correcting when she was little than my other 4 children combined. I want to make certain you understand my definition of correcting. I do not mean beating or whipping or bruising or hitting with a fist or belt or any other object. I mean giving a light swat on the behind when needed or a consequence of some sort. She had 'time-outs' and she would lose a privilege or a favorite possession and still does.

Before she was diagnosed, I would see her unwillingness to cooperate as pure obstinance. The words: sensory integration, motor planning skills, obsessive behaviors and many others were not in my vocabulary. I had never even heard those terms.

I expected her to be quiet in church, be polite to people, use her best manners, strive hard to accomplish things and to do as I asked. In retrospect, that's a pretty intimidating list for any child, especially one with special needs.

Kalisha was a good kid, not because she was punished but because she was friendly, curious and eager to please…most of the time. She did, however, have a stubborn streak a mile wide and although there were times it made me furious, there were also times when I believe it was that stubborn tenacity that helped her accomplish a lot of things.

She was a great imitator. I remember her sitting on the living room floor, working on something. I asked her several times to stand up, please. She ignored me and refused to stand. I gently grabbed a handful of her *mass of hair* and slowly started tugging upward. She managed to get to her feet rather quickly. A week later, when she was at her sister's house, she wanted Kendra to get something for her. (Kendra has a mass of curls, also) Evidently, Kendra wasn't standing up fast enough for Kalisha, so she grabbed a handful of hair and started tugging upward. I was troubled by this although I believe it worked for her too as I heard about it later when Kendra laughingly questioned my parenting techniques. I did discuss this with Kalisha. I did not want her to think it was permissible to 'help' people stand up by using their hair.

As an adolescent, there was an instance when Kalisha was giving me a hard time about something. She suddenly stopped, looked at me, and very seriously asked, "Am I doing that because I'm autistic or am I just being a brat?" Ah…therein lies the question. It is sometimes difficult to discern what the behavior is attributed to.

There is no such thing as a 'perfect child'… typical or non-typical. It is very hard to determine the cause of some behaviors. It is also easy to make excuses and say, "My child can't help it. That behavior is due to his/her disability." While it may be true, it is still our responsibility as parents and mentors to help them behave in a way that is acceptable in society. It may seem unfortunate, undeserving and prejudicial, but society as a whole, does not tolerate obnoxious behavior, even from a special needs child.

A year ago, my 18-year-old granddaughter came to live at our house. Kalisha was used to having the shower at the time she needed it and suddenly, she had to share the shower and adjust her 'times.' Was it easy for her? No. She argued, complained, and had a fit when her schedule was upset. My first reaction was to make sure she got her time and Elizabeth would have to work around it; after all, Kalisha was the one who lived by a specific routine and schedule and was not very flexible.

I realized, with the help of Kalisha's Behavioral Consultant, this could be a great learning experience for her. Barring an accident of some kind, it is fairly certain I will die before Kalisha. She will most likely live in an apartment with another special needs adult. Wouldn't it be better for her to learn to be a bit flexible *now* rather than *then*? I thought so. Elizabeth and Kalisha had many morning arguments, but eventually learned to accommodate each other's schedules.

She is not a child any longer, but occasionally, she is still disciplined. I will listen to her arguing with me for just so long. When I see that trying to reason with her is pointless, I send her to her room.

There were 2 phrases I was taught to use when she was quite young:

#1 That is not acceptable behavior.
#2 These are your consequences.

Kalisha learned those phrases well enough that she would repeat them when talking to her dolls or pets. I still use them today. She still has consequences today. If she doesn't keep a commitment she has made she loses her phone and computer for 24 hours. She understands that and rarely avoids any commitment.

I believe it is my job as a parent to teach kindness, respect, sharing, listening, manners, being able to function outside her comfort zone and just plain civility, in order to prepare her for living in society. I also know there are some things she can't control and some behaviors she is continually working on. Kalisha, like all of us, is still a work in progress.

Sensory Issues

PROBABLY EVERY HUMAN has a sensory issue of some kind; we either don't recognize it or we've never identified it as such. My son hated any shirt or sweater that even remotely resembled a turtleneck, one daughter had an aversion to tags in the back of her clothing. The difference between most of us and an individual with autism is the *number* of things that cause sensory problems and the *severity* of them.

When Kalisha was young, I was, *again*, unaware of the terminology: sensory issues. I knew there were things that bothered Kalisha but I usually tried to avoid those particular things. She does not eat any meat in 'chunks.' Examples: She will eat shaved ham, but not a piece of a baked ham. She will eat shaved turkey, not a piece of turkey. Cheeseburgers are the love of her life, but don't ask her to eat a steak or piece of roast beef. When I make any pasta casserole which contains meat, I serve hers before I add the meat. She refuses to eat chicken noodle soup unless I remove the pieces of chicken, which we know are microscopic. She doesn't like chicken in any form, other than an occasional Chicken McNugget. (She is a McDonald's connoisseur...that might qualify as an oxymoron)

She doesn't wear hose or leggings. Sweatshirts are okay but no sweaters. Positively no turtlenecks or any clothing that is form-fitting.

It was a struggle to get her to wear a bra when she first needed one. She complained daily about the *feel* of it. She only wears a certain cut of underwear and a certain type of socks. Sometimes things I think will bother her, don't seem to. The heel of her sock is usually on the top of her foot, which would be uncomfortable to me. Obviously, it doesn't bother her at all.

She hates the smell of cigarette smoke but likes a campfire's smell. She never goes swimming because she can't handle the smell of lake water and hates the chlorine smell of a pool or hot tub.

For a very long time, she would only take a bath because the spray hitting her skin in a shower drove her crazy. She did overcome that one issue and can take a shower now.

She doesn't like being too hot or too cold. Most people don't like those temperature changes, but she is much more sensitive to them than the average person. You are probably wondering why we live in Indiana. I wonder that too, on occasion.

A friend coaxed her into having fake nails. I knew she was in trouble the minute she walked in the door. They looked very nice, but the length was extremely disturbing to her.

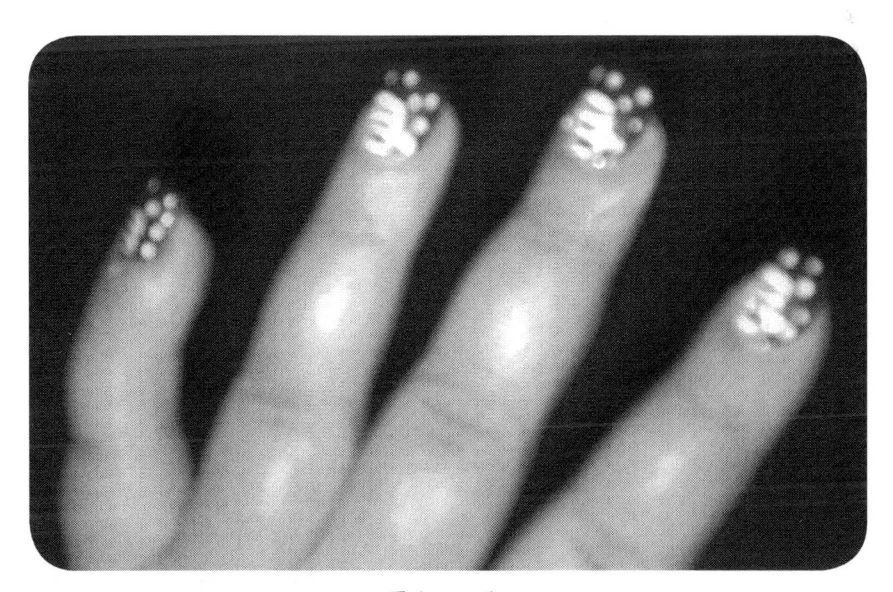

Fake nails

After calling several nail salons to find the best way to remove them, I had a brainstorm. I used nail clippers and snipped off the ends. Problem solved. She still had beautiful nails and they didn't bother her.

Kalisha doesn't like the feel of anything on her face. Due to her light sleep patterns and snoring, her doctor suggested a sleep apnea test. She was adamant she was not going to wear anything on her face. I talked her into at least taking the test so we would know. Foolish, foolish me. The doctor convinced her it was an easy test and all she had to do was sleep. Right.

We arrived at the sleep clinic in the early evening. Kalisha gets the prize for asking the most questions of the technicians who were hooking her up to all the wires. They gave me permission to stay with her. I thought I would sleep in the recliner provided. What was I thinking? This is a sample of the running dialogue for the next 8 hours:

"I can't sleep like this."

"I never sleep on my back."

"What time is it?"

"These wires bother me."

"My back hurts."

"What time is it?"

"I can't sleep on my back anymore."

"I want to go home to my bed."

"I'm thirsty."

"I'm cold."

"I don't want them to watch me sleep."

"What time is it?"

""I'm not going to wear anything on my face anyway."

"I want to roll on my side."

"My back hurts."

"What time is it?"

After several hours of this, *I* was the one asking, 'What time is it?'

She (we) did finally make it through the night. Her doctor called to say they didn't get very good test results (surprise, surprise) and should schedule another one. The chances of that happening were somewhere between zero and non-existent. They would have to use what they had. The results indicated 'severe sleep apnea' and she definitely needed to wear the apparatus at night. Kalisha listened, nodded her head and on the way to the car, stated emphatically, "I'm not wearing anything on my face It will bother me and I will never go to sleep."

We have reached an agreement. Until she agrees to wear it or they invent something less annoying to her sensory issues, she will continue to snore and sleep as she always has. If it causes her to die young, we will meet in heaven.

Pain Tolerance

I DON'T RECALL WHEN I first realized Kalisha's tolerance for pain was different than my first four children. She seldom cried about a skinned knee, a bruised elbow or any other childhood mishap. She would scratch a mosquito bite until it bled. When I told her to stop, she seemed oblivious to the fact it was bleeding.

She had surgery on her eye when she was eighteen months old. I don't know if that surgery is particularly painful, but I believe most children would fuss and cry due to the anesthetic, the eye patch and just being in the hospital. She didn't.

When she was small and in the barn with me, the goats would often step on her toes or jostle her around. The kid goats might knock her flat if it was feeding time. She didn't seem to notice if she was hurt. I would see a bruise when giving her a bath, but she could never recall how or when it happened.

If she had a hangnail or a toenail with a jagged edge, she would pick at it until she could pull it off. She would show it to me after the fact. It would be bleeding and make me hurt just to look at it. My wise friend and mentor explained to me how the rough edge on a nail was more bothersome to Kalisha than any pain she might cause to herself. That was frightening to me. I could only imagine the amount of damage she could inflict on herself before it became too painful.

When Kalisha was in kindergarten, she walked down our snowy driveway to the bus. I walked with her but she didn't want to hold my hand. She slipped on a slick spot and fell down. I helped her up, brushed the snow off and asked if she was okay. She nodded yes and boarded the bus for the ride to school.

The school called around lunch time. They were concerned about Kalisha's arm because she couldn't seem to hold her lunch tray. I picked her up immediately and took her to the emergency room where her arm was x-rayed. It was broken in 2 places and required a cast for 6 weeks. On my way out, I picked up my "Mother of the Year" award.

We had frost-free water hydrants in the barn. These had a large metal handle, which you pulled down to shut off the flow of water. She was holding on to one of the pipes when I pulled the handle down and pinched her finger between two pieces of metal. I didn't even realize it had happened. She just stood there looking at me. When I saw what had happened, I finally freed her finger, which was broken, of course.

Her fear of hot things began when she was twelve years old and riding in the front seat of the pick-up truck with me. The truck had a manual transmission with the gearshift on the floor. I asked her to hold my travel mug full of hot coffee while I shifted into the next gear. The truck hit a bump in the road and the lid on my cup, which obviously wasn't fastened well, came off. The hot coffee splashed on her. That time she did say, "Yikes. That is really hot." I immediately turned around and went home because I knew if she said it hurt, she probably had a huge blister. She did.

When Kalisha was in her early twenties, she wanted to have breast reduction surgery. Her breasts were heavy enough to cause grooves in her shoulders and make her stand hunched over. The insurance company agreed and it was scheduled. After surgery, she was prescribed Vicodin for pain. Kalisha hates to be put to sleep or take any medication that will cause her to be drowsy. She took one Vicodin when we arrived home. It made her a little loopy, but she remembered the feeling and didn't like it. When it was time for the next pill, she refused. "I'll take a Tylenol but I don't want any more of those pain pills."

The surgery was quite extensive and I'm certain I would have wanted a pain pill, but she never took another.

She still will 'pick' at a fingernail or toenail, but has gotten much better about telling me it needs to be clipped before she just rips it off and takes a chunk of skin with it.

If she complains of a stomach ache or a headache, I take notice, immediately. I took her to the emergency room when she was complaining of a severe pain in her chest. It turned out to be indigestion, but I couldn't take the chance when she was specific about a pain. If Kalisha complains that something hurts, I am certain it would be excruciating for anyone else.

Aw-w-w-w POOP

I promise not to be gross, but if this is TMI (too much information) for you, just skip this chapter and move to the next one.

To state Kalisha had bowel problems from the beginning would be putting it mildly. As soon as she began eating solid food, she would usually have a bowel movement only every couple of days. I found this unusual, but when I questioned the pediatrician, he gave me the standard line, "Well, all kids are different and she just isn't a child who needs to go every day."

Kalisha had 4 older siblings and I was well aware of the fact that all children are different; however, it still did not seem normal to me. Being from a DON'T QUESTION THE EXPERTS kind of upbringing, I took his word for it. After all, he was the one with the degree, right?

The problem did not go away. When it was time for potty training, she would set on her potty chair and strain until her face turned purple, but she could not go.

I was so naïve and uninformed, I didn't know where or how to research bowel movements. I had no idea it was a common trait of nearly all special needs individuals. I had never heard the term, 'motor planning' or the reason many of them have difficulty with elimination is due to a lack of motor planning skills. They do not feel the urge to push and when they do push, it isn't with the correct muscles, so nothing happens. Kalisha was 14 years old before I learned those facts. That is a lot of years of poop frustration.

When Kalisha had not gone for several days, I would resort to using a baby enema. She hated it (Of course, she did. I never heard of anyone who was thrilled about having an enema). The thought of having a BM became so traumatic for her, she would take her potty chair and try to find a hiding spot.

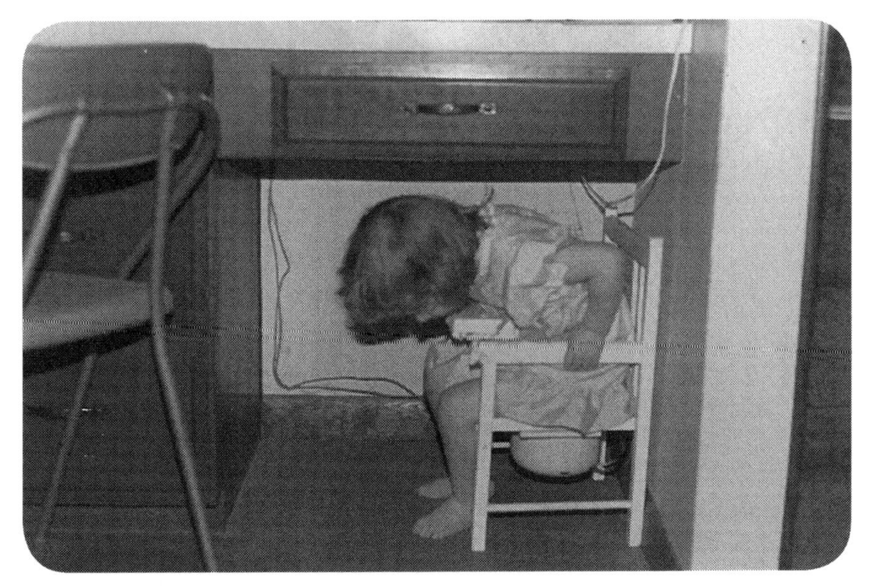

Hiding with her potty chair

I did take her to a new pediatrician. He had the 'miracle cure.' Yes, finally! He prescribed Colace and mineral oil to be taken every day. That makes you gag just thinking about it, doesn't it? Kalisha swallowed the nasty concoction every day even though it was revolting. Anything was better than an enema. It did work - sort of.

One day after she had used the toilet, I noticed pools of oil floating on top of the water. I definitely was not a doctor, but I knew if her colon was coated with so much mineral oil it was running out of her, her colon was certainly not absorbing any nutrients she needed. Okay, we stopped that treatment immediately and found a new pediatrician.

The next stop was a gastroenterologist. I tried to explain to him a rectal exam would be totally out of the question for Kalisha. I asked if he could check her with an x-ray or perhaps admit her to a hospital as an out-patient and mildly sedate her as they do for a colonoscopy. He, being *god* and all, insisted he knew how to check Kalisha without any trauma to her. Like an idiot, I acquiesced and trusted him. (I'm a slow learner, obviously)

Needless to say, it was *not* a good experience. And, after all that, all he could tell me was she had an obstruction of feces in her colon. NO KIDDING! I never took her back to him, but the problem was still unresolved. She developed fissures around her rectum and hemorrhoids due to the size of her excrement when she was finally able to go.

Kalisha missed many fun things because she was miserable. The constipation would give her an upset stomach and cramps. She would be very pale and not want to leave the couch. We went on a Disney cruise, but due to feeling bad, she chose to stay in the cabin instead of visiting an island. We were at Mall of America and she asked to stay in the hotel room instead of sightseeing. Pooping or not pooping ruled her life.

Eventually, Kalisha stumbled upon her own solution to the problem. This worked for her, but I want to emphasize I am not stating it will work for anyone else. She began to eat a bowl of Raisin Bran for breakfast every morning; she drank apple juice and ate at least one raw apple every day. She still struggles a little, but does go regularly. I don't believe her colon will ever return to normal size, so, at our house, the plunger is our best friend.

This whole scenario falls into the "Why didn't somebody tell me?" category. I take full responsibility for being naïve, uninformed and unquestioning. Since I thought my child was the only one with this particular problem, it certainly wasn't a topic of conversation when I talked to other parents. I realize it was 29 years ago, autism and special needs were not on the radar like they are today, but surely, in the 14 years before Kalisha found her own solution, one of the experts would have been aware of the connection between intestinal problems and individuals with special needs.

As *enlightened* as I became, I was still shocked just a few years ago, when I had a conversation with the administrator of a large special needs community. She was in charge of many group homes, and the employees there. Because constipation is such a common issue affecting nearly all the clients at the residences, she laughingly told me any new employee has to pass the 'plunger usage test' before they can work for her.

That fact eluded me for way too long and I am sorry it took me so long to be a better advocate for Kalisha in this area of her health needs.

Choose Wisely

I WAS STUNNED WHEN someone advised me to schedule an interview appointment before selecting a health care provider of any kind. I had never conducted an interview with any doctor, dentist or specialist in my lifetime.

Part of my difficulty with the idea stemmed from the fact when I was growing up in a small rural community, there was only one doctor and dentist available; no choosing was necessary. I also grew up in an era where any person of authority: doctors, lawyers, teachers, clergy, law enforcement, supposedly knew what they were talking about and their opinions were not questioned. I had to lose that mindset if I wanted to be an advocate for Kalisha, but it was difficult. Of course, I had to learn the hard way.

When Kalisha was born, she was under the care of a group of pediatricians. I certainly had not interviewed any of them. Why would I? I was going to have a perfectly healthy baby and all I needed was a doctor to provide routine health care like I had with my other children. I started looking for a new doctor when I realized they had not been truthful with me and when her main pediatrician advised me to place her in an institution because she would never progress any further, physically or mentally. She was less than two years old and there was no diagnosis of any kind at that point.

I switched her records to a general practitioner in the small community where we lived. I liked and trusted him and he did well with Kalisha.

After I saw her ever-increasing number of health problems and what I thought were the symptoms of autism, I thought we should switch to a pediatrician.

I scheduled an interview with a husband/wife pediatric team. I asked if they had other patients with autism. He looked at her and said, "We see that one kid who wears a helmet, right?" Okay, I crossed them off the list.

After much praying and asking other parents, we found a doctor who was fantastic. She was a general practitioner and she and Kalisha had an awesome rapport. She understood Kalisha; she teased her, she knew her likes, dislikes and peculiarities. Then she moved to another part of the state. What a loss that was.

We finally chose another family practitioner. This experience was not good at all. In fact, it was totally the opposite. She could never remember Kalisha's name or even one small thing about her. She referred us to a specialist for *everything*. A hangnail would require seeing a dermatologist.

She did one thing to our benefit; she sent Kalisha to an OB-GYN for exams and tests. Kalisha absolutely loved her. She was soft-spoken, understanding, had a sense of humor, remembered Kalisha and related to her. You know she is awesome if she can hang in there with Kalisha while talking her through a total exam, including a pap smear.

When Kalisha began having grand mal seizures, we were referred to a neurologist. He had the personality of a doorknob. He experimented with several different meds and dosages, but the seizures continued. I made an appointment with a neurologist at Riley Children's Hospital in Indianapolis, a huge complex. The first 5 minutes of the first visit, I knew we had the right doctor. He not only found the correct medication with the first try, he was interested in Kalisha, the person. He told her about his experience of seeing the singing group, In-Sync, when he was in Brazil. He endeared himself to her forever, as she was a big In-Sync fan at that time and he took the time to know that about her.

Kalisha needed to see a gastroenterologist. I knew this was going to be unbelievably difficult even if she liked him. She didn't and neither did I. He was pretty certain he was god and knew everything about her, even though he did not listen to anything I said. That was a one visit encounter, also. It should have been a *no-visit* encounter.

When it came to ophthalmologists, we got it right the first time. Kalisha saw a charming, sensitive competent doctor for her eyes. He surgically corrected one eye when she was very young and examined her eyes annually until she was an adult. When she was young, he would make 'Donald Duck' noises to keep her entertained during the exams. Today, due to his care, she has no fear or hesitancy when it comes to eye exams.

The right dentist is more difficult to find. We started with a local dentist. Kalisha didn't really misbehave or thrash around, but she did refuse to open her mouth; something that is a tad bit necessary at the dentist's office. He was honest enough to suggest we find someone else, as he didn't feel he would be able to deal with Kalisha. I appreciated his honesty. Eventually, through recommendations from acquaintances, we found a pediatric dentist. He was the dentist for residents of several group homes so I was pretty sure he could convince Kalisha to open her mouth. She saw him until she reached the age of eighteen and he could no longer keep her as a patient.

As an adult, she saw one dentist for one visit and refused to go back. I met him and his staff. They all seemed very nice to me, but she would not return, even though she couldn't tell me why. I didn't force the issue. I assumed she had some radar I didn't have. Instead we looked for another one. Kalisha had her heart set on going to a large dental practice she saw advertised on television. They were extremely kind, patient and friendly. Those are all required qualities in my book. The dentist/owner always took the time to work on Kalisha's teeth, himself.

At one point, Kalisha required the services of an orthodontist. This was the ultimate great experience. It was a large practice, but the staff made a point to remember her name and the things she was interested in. They would have actual conversations with her. The doctor would make certain he personally was the one who worked on her. She loved him and his assistants. He fitted her with a 'Herbst appliance' nicknamed a 'herbie.' It fit onto her bottom jaw and forced it forward. She tolerated braces on her upper teeth to straighten them. I would never, in a million years, have believed she would keep the 'herbie' in her mouth or accept braces; too many sensory issues and inconveniences involved. But she did. The atmosphere at the office and the employees were the ones who made it happen.

The one thing all of the *successful* doctors, counselors and specialists had in common was the ability to actually *know* Kalisha. They related to her, enjoyed her and had conversations with her; like a real person. That's something we all want, isn't it?

Mental Health Professionals

WHILE I LABOR under the delusion that mental health counselors should have their ducks in a row; it seems, they are just as prone to mistakes and bad judgment as every other type of professional. Having said that, it took me a few experiences to know I had to continue searching for the perfect match for Kalisha.

To tell the truth, I can't even remember 'why' it was suggested she see a counselor the first time. I certainly can remember the experience, though.

I had no idea how to go about finding the right one, so I did what I had done in the past when looking for medical professionals: I asked friends and acquaintances. That was tricky when talking about mental health because no one wanted to admit their child actually needed to see a professional. We finally made an appointment with a woman who was highly recommended by various agencies. She was supposedly very good with mentally challenged individuals.

Kalisha was in her late teens, chronologically, but probably only twelve or thirteen, in actuality. The first visit, the counselor talked to me alone for the first half-hour. She asked questions and scribbled notes for the entire hour and never spoke to Kalisha. The next visit, I waited in the waiting room while she saw Kalisha. On the way home, I didn't ask about their conversation, but I did ask what she thought about the session. In her very candid way, she said, "I don't think I like her and I know she doesn't like me."

That was not a good omen, but we persevered; after all, wasn't she highly recommended? The next visit, I ran a few errands while Kalisha was with her. When I picked her up, she said she wasn't supposed to come back…ever.

"Really?" I asked. "Did she say why?"

Kalisha said, "Yeah. She said I needed to take a shower more often. I was making the waiting room smell like sweat."

I was furious. Kalisha may have needed a few more pointers about hygiene (remember, I said she a young teen, emotionally) but she certainly did not smell and we both knew she never worked hard enough to work up a sweat.

That was our first foray into the land of counseling; not a pleasant one.

Several years later, after some harrowing experiences, it was suggested she see a counselor for PTSD (post-traumatic stress disorder) symptoms. Again, we went fishing for the right one. It is difficult to find someone who is qualified as a counselor and is also familiar with the behaviors and thought processes of a person with autism.

The first agency sent us to a very nice middle-aged woman. After 2 visits, she asked if we would agree to see a young counselor who had experience with persons on the spectrum, as she herself, didn't feel qualified. We agreed. Kalisha came home from the first visit and reported the counselor was texting the entire hour. I suggested perhaps she was taking notes on her phone. Kalisha told me she was texting her friend in Chicago and making plans for the weekend. Not cool. Obviously, this young woman didn't think an autistic person would care if she were being ignored. I reported her actions to the man in charge of the agency (never received a response) and we moved on once again.

The next counselor, again, was highly recommended. There was one problem: he was visually impaired. I didn't realize how much that fact would affect their sessions. For Kalisha, it was indeed a problem. She liked him, but never really opened up to him. Perhaps his lack of sight should not have made any difference but she didn't feel as though he was listening to her if he couldn't actually *see* her.

Through some recommendations from her case manager and a behaviorist, we found the woman who was an answer to prayer. She suggested a 90-day trial period to ascertain if Kalisha liked *her* and if she liked Kalisha and thought she could help her. I was totally impressed by that.

The first thing that was done was a complete psychological evaluation by the psychiatrist in charge of this office. He was the one who added the Asperger's Syndrome label to the autism and mental retardation. I questioned how it was possible to have both those labels. To me it seemed Asperger's indicated high functioning while the mildly mentally challenged diagnosis was a polar opposite. The autism label is a huge umbrella for many symptoms and behaviors and although Kalisha was high-functioning in many areas, she was also still mentally challenged in many others. I did not realize a person could have both autism and Asperger's. He explained it to me in terminology I could understand.

I read chapters about Asperger's, nodding my head at each new description. I recognized so many things describing Kalisha accurately. Then I would switch to the autism section of the book. She and many of her actions were described there, also. The mental retardation didn't fit anywhere in the equation. She is really an enigma. She doesn't fit in any of the boxes. Males are much more likely to have autism than females. Many of the autism and Asperger's symptoms overlap and she meets the criteria for both. Due to some events in Kalisha's life, she was also diagnosed with PTSD (post-traumatic stress disorder). These events are detailed in another chapter.

This time, everything fell in place. Kalisha liked Riki and I felt Riki genuinely liked Kalisha. They had a great rapport. Riki was not a pushover for some of Kalisha's ideas but she did always talk her through her problems. She allowed Kalisha to express the events of the past year without anyone else's input. Kalisha trusted her and was comfortable talking to her. Riki saw Kalisha every 2 weeks for eighteen months.

She would occasionally ask me to join them for part of a session; always with Kalisha's permission. When she felt Kalisha was in a good place, psychologically and emotionally, Riki cut her loose with the understanding that she would always be available if Kalisha ever felt as though life was becoming overwhelming again. It was a comfort to know that.

Although I stated I would not give advice, here it is. DO NOT give up until you find the professional that you and your child are comfortable with. I know it is always a struggle when it comes to insurance, co-pays, changing locations and requesting records, but when you find the right one, it is all worth it.

Seizures, Seizures, Seizures

KALISHA'S FIRST SEIZURE occurred when she was only 6 months old. It was a petit mal, or small seizure. Her eyes rolled back in her head and her entire body went limp. It scared me to death. I called the EMS; they took her to the hospital where they kept her overnight for observation. Although they found nothing abnormal, the doctor instructed me to keep a journal of any seizure activity I observed, no matter how small.

Now that I knew what I was looking for, I would see her have very brief 'losses of connection' which were only a few seconds in duration. Her eyes would have a vacant stare but it disappeared so quickly, I was never certain if I had actually seen it or not.

One stormy night when she was fourteen, she came into my bedroom in the middle of the night and asked if she could sleep with me because of the severe thunderstorm. I awoke a few hours later to violent shaking. The entire bed seemed to be moving.

I'm not the most functional person when I'm suddenly awakened, so it took me a minute to roll over and realize it was Kalisha who was shaking uncontrollably. Her eyes were rolled so far back into her head, they were no longer visible and I could not make her stop shaking. A million things flashed through my mind...everything I had ever heard about seizures;

whether true or old wives' tales. While I was still contemplating what to do, the shaking stopped and she seemed to be sleeping peacefully.

A frantic call brought an ambulance and paramedics to the house. While I was talking to them in the kitchen, describing the incident in detail, Kalisha came walking out, looked at them and calmly asked, "What are they doing here?" She had absolutely no recollection of what had transpired.

They examined her and advised me to take her to the hospital for observation. They also instructed me on what to do if it happened again. I should make certain she was in a comfortable position where she couldn't harm herself when flailing around and wait for it to pass. They assured me she would not die from a seizure as long as she didn't hit her head or otherwise injure herself as she fell. That was at least a little bit comforting.

After her night in the hospital, she was scheduled to see a neurologist. He prescribed a 'trial' medication. It didn't work. She continued to have seizures. There were never any warning signs that I could discern. Each time, she would just sink to the floor and begin jerking violently. On one occasion, she ended up with a painful rug burn on her knee where it was rubbing on the carpet with each jerk. I didn't realize it was happening at the time. She would be unbelievably tired after each episode. I would cover her and let her sleep wherever she was.

No one, including the neurologist, ever suggested a connection between autism and seizures. She had the usual battery of tests: MRI, EEG and an attempted 'sleep deprivation" EEG. That one didn't work so well as she refused to try and go to sleep. I believe she was frightened of what might happen if she did.

After several trial and error medications, I asked that her case be transferred to Riley Children's Hospital in Indianapolis. I couldn't continue to watch while the neurologist kept experimenting. This was my little girl having seizures, not some actress in a movie.

I felt better after our very first visit to Riley. Her neurologist was wonderful. He actually talked to her and conversed about things she might like; Back Street Boys, In-Sync (he wasn't clairvoyant, just observant..she was wearing a T-shirt with In-Sync on it), books, school. AND he explained to us what was going on, in a few words. Autism hit puberty and bam!..seizures. It didn't happen to all children with autism, but many. He prescribed a medication that worked on the first try. Thank you, God. It took a little tweaking to get the dosage right, but no more grand mal seizures.

Each time we returned for a follow-up visit, Kalisha would ask, "Do I have to take these pills for the rest of my life?" He would tell her he honestly didn't know. She might outgrow the seizures, but for right then, it was working.

We found the answer to her question through my misunderstanding. Her neurologist asked that we bring her to Riley for an early morning EEG. We went the night before and stayed at a hotel because her test was scheduled for 7 a.m. I thought his nurse had told me to *withhold* her medication for 2 doses before the test. WRONG!! Kalisha got out of bed in the morning and immediately went to the floor, hitting her face on the footboard on the way down and had a full-blown seizure. Do you have any idea how much blood can be sprayed around when a person is jerking that violently?

It looked like a CSI crime scene. Before we left the hotel, I called the front desk to explain what had happened so housekeeping wouldn't think someone had been murdered in our room.

It doesn't do much for you getting the 'parent of the year' award when you bring your child in for a test, her face is black and blue and they have to x-ray her for broken facial bones before the test. There was one positive that came out of it; we now knew she couldn't stop taking the medication.

A few years ago, Kalisha had to find a new family doctor. The first thing this doctor wanted to do was change the seizure meds. Her reasoning was that Tegretol was an old medicine and perhaps we should try something newer. My thought was, "If it ain't broke, don't fix it." Thankfully, she was sent to a local neurologist (she had graduated from Riley Hospital, due to her age) and he agreed with me. She is still on the same medication today. Does she still need it now that she's older? I don't know, but I'm not willing to risk a seizure to find out.

Living In Two Worlds

KALISHA HAS ALWAYS had to maneuver in several different worlds. In many instances, she is forced to live in the world of her chronological age. She had to attend school and be in the age-appropriate classroom, doing the age-appropriate activities, even if she didn't understand lesson concepts or wasn't able to perform in gym class.

In third grade, she evidently was bored one day, so she pulled her shirt up to her chin, exposing her bare chest, of course. The teacher was appalled, the children were laughing at her and Kalisha was enjoying the attention.

If she had been in preschool, the teacher would have told her to put her shirt down, the kids probably wouldn't have cared or they would have all followed her lead and the entire classroom would have been showing off their bare chests. In reality, she was a 5-year-old acting out but living in a 9-year-old world. The *world* expected her to behave as if she were 9 years old.

Her body didn't wait until she was old enough to understand what was happening before she started having her periods. I did prepare her and we talked about every aspect of what was going to happen, but she still was not really prepared for it. She would say, "Yeah, okay," and move on to something else, because she was really only 9 or 10, developmentally, instead of 14, chronologically.

It would break my heart to see her trying to fit in with the 9-year-old neighborhood girls when she was actually 18 years old. She wanted to play school and tag or color on the sidewalk with chalk. They would let her play, but she could never be the 'teacher,' always the follower. When they played tag, she was always 'it.'

Playing with much younger children

I wanted to tell her to come inside and not play with them, but I realized as I watched, she was enjoying herself. Should I deprive her of that little bit of fun because *I* was embarrassed?

When she purchases a Build-a-Bear animal, the other customers who are 'making' their animal are always young children. She looks out of place, but she doesn't seem to mind. Should I?

An example of her 2 worlds: She is planning a party for her 30th birthday. She wants the mascots of her 2 favorite sports teams to be at the party. That is Kalisha, the little girl. She has reserved the mascots, found pictures of cakes decorated as she wants, reserved the room at our church, and found invitations, all via internet, phone or e-mail, without any help from me. That is Kalisha, the adult.

Kalisha's ability to switch from one mindset to another is a marvel to me, but I think it must be difficult in many aspects, for her.

She loves country music. When she attended a Kenny Chesney country music concert with a girlfriend, she took pictures of the two of them posed at a Hooters booth with orange foam hats on their heads. When she came home and showed me the pictures, I asked if she knew what Hooters was. She said, "Yeah, it's a restaurant where the waitresses are almost naked and I don't want to go there, but I liked the hats." Okay, the child liked the hats, the adult liked the concert.

She enjoys and collects the American Girl dolls, as her budget will allow. She has them on shelves in her room, she has read all of the stories about each one and knows the time period of each one. She has learned a lot of history facts from these books. She doesn't play with them because 'pretending' does not come easily to Kalisha; she just owns them.

For a long period of time, she watched every Disney movie and owned most of them on VHS. Several years ago she began replacing the VHS tapes with the DVD version. I suggested she not replace some of the more 'kiddie' ones, such as Winnie-the Pooh and Eeyore. She looked at me as though I had just landed from some other planet. Of course she was going to replace them. She enjoyed them.

As a senior in high school, she went to the prom with a young man, but the next day, was watching a Disney movie. She is a huge fan of the Indianapolis Colts football team. She totally understands the positions and plays and never misses a game on television, but will read a *Mary Kate and Ashley* book when the game is over.

Kalisha and I went to see Disney on Ice when it came to Fort Wayne. As an adult, I enjoyed it, because the colors and costumes were stunning. Kalisha, however, felt like she shouldn't tell anyone she enjoyed it or that she bought a coloring book while we were there. "Why?" I asked. "There are many adults here, a lot of them without any children. What's the difference between them and you?"

"It's different," she said. "If they tell people they went to Disney On Ice or they bought a coloring book, people will say how cute that is. But if I tell people I went, they will think I am a kid and will never grow up and I can *only* like Disney."

How can someone who is mentally challenged and autistic be so insightful? It seemed like pretty mature thinking to me, but I understood what she was saying. I totally 'got' it. And she was right in her assessment of that whole situation.

Many times, lately, she has used the term, mature. She will say, "That was a mature thing for me to do, huh, Mom?" or "I'm starting to act more mature, huh?"

I'm not sure if she really wants to be more mature or thinks that is how she is *supposed* to be and act. It must be hard to have to think about it all the time. And rather sad, too, I think.

As her mother, I live in two worlds, also. I want her to have the independence she strives for and be able to make her own decisions. Quite often I will tell her she needs to handle a situation by herself.

On the other hand, I can transform into "Mama Bear' quite easily. I become angry and upset when some of her girlfriends treat her badly or hurt her feelings or if I overhear a snide conversation or see a snub by a group of girls. My first instinct is to jump right in and 'fix' it. Most of the time, the comments bother me infinitely more than they bother her. Perhaps that's why I feel the need to take over and be angry *for* her. She doesn't see the snubs or understand the comments are derogatory. I should leave it alone. I'm still working on that.

There was an occasion when Kalisha was supposed to attend a ballgame with two adults named Lori and Sarah and several younger children. When Lori thought Sarah wasn't going to be able to accompany them, she insisted I go along. I had other plans. Kalisha sized up the situation and told me, "Lori's afraid of me, isn't she?" I had the exact same thought, so we discussed it. I tried to help her see when people are unfamiliar with her and don't know what she might say or do, they become insecure and that turns into fear.

I was blown away by Kalisha's perceptiveness. She understood but she also said, "That hurts my feelings." I'm sure it did. It hurt mine, too.

Fascinations and Fun Destinations

KALISHA HAS SOME major obsessions that are usually attached to certain people; but she also has some minor ones, which I refer to as fascinations instead of obsessions. These don't rule her life but are always present in her subconscious.

Limousines are one of those fascinations. She has been fascinated by limos since she was a little girl. I have no idea why or how it started; nor do I care. It's a relatively harmless interest…unless she decides to carjack one someday.

While traveling, she can spot a limousine from a mile away. She especially likes the trip to her aunt's house, near Chicago. On the interstate approaching O'Hare airport, they are more than plentiful. Immaculate shiny black ones, dazzling white ones, some longer than others and some are SUV limousines. She comments about all of them.

When we visited San Francisco, there was a long, black one parked along a street near the waterfront. We were walking past when she suddenly asked if she could talk to the driver. He was standing by the side of the limo, obviously waiting on his passengers. He not only answered her questions, he opened the doors and let her peek inside. She was only 9 years old at the time.

When she was approaching her 16th birthday, I tried to think of something special to do. After all, 16 is sort of a milestone. I had a brilliant idea. I hired a limo to pick her up at church, where I was employed at the time. The first ride was for her and all the staff at the church.

Birthday limo picking friends up at school

Twelve people climbed inside, enjoying sodas and snacks with some sticking their heads up through the sunroof. The driver drove around town for some time. After he brought them back, they went to 3 different schools and picked up some of her friends. The one parochial school had a 'car line' where all drivers line up to grab their children. It takes quite a long time, but Kalisha loved every minute of it. The other parents and the waiting students were very curious about the limousine waiting in line with the other cars. The niece they picked up was having a great time telling everyone she was getting into that limo.

After he had corralled his passengers from 3 different schools, the driver drove around town for a while and then ended the trip at Pizza Hut, where I met them. We celebrated with pizza and cake. That was one of her best birthday surprises.

She is also fascinated with The Weather Channel. When she was younger, she could watch it for hours, even though it was quite repetitive. She didn't seem to mind.

I made the decision when she was young to allow her to explore the things that fascinated her, like the limos, if it could be accomplished. I tried to broaden her world with various experiences when possible.

She participated in Special Olympics one time and was a 4-H member for 10 years. She also enjoyed therapeutic horseback riding lessons for 2 years.

Receiving her medal at Special Olympics

Showing goats in 4-H

She liked all things Disney, so we attended a local production of a Cinderella ballet. I neglected to warn her about ballets. Her comment at intermission was, "Are they ever going to talk?" We saw live productions at our local library, theater and art cinema. Many times some of the actors were friends, so it was much more interesting for Kalisha.

We had an incredible opportunity to spend 3 days at Disney World and 3 days on a Disney cruise. She had a wonderful time; securing autographs from every Disney character she could find.

Kalisha accompanied us on a business trip to San Francisco. She was fascinated by the cable cars. One of her favorite television series, 'Full House' was filmed there, so she felt like she was familiar with the area. The plane ride, the ocean, the vendors and the musicians on the street were all new experiences for her.

We took a Christmas shopping trip to Chicago on a bus. While there, we visited the American Girl Store and ate at The Rainforest Café.

Visiting the Rainforest Café and the American Girl store

When there was a chance to take a short ride on a steam locomotive, we did. We rode a passenger train to Chicago to visit relatives, and we ate in the dining car.

She made several flights to Houston to visit her sister, Kari and her family. I made sure they were non-stop flights and stayed with her until she got on the plane. Kari would then meet her at the gate when she arrived in Texas. She has toured the Alamo and taken a boat ride down the river in San Antonio, Texas.

She has been on numerous car trips to other states to watch her niece, Lynley, play volleyball.

None of these activities, with the exception of the Disney trip, were expensive. They were worth the time and effort to allow Kalisha to experience a world outside her everyday life. They were priceless experiences for her and she has wonderful memories.

Strengths and Weaknesses

I asked Kalisha to list her strengths and weaknesses, as she sees them. She thought about it for awhile and gave me a fairly comprehensive and accurate list. She is quite perceptive, about herself and others. That is a strength, most of the time.

Kalisha was 12 when her sister and her husband lived at our house for a few months. She and her brother-in-law's relationship was not a *mutual admiration society*. One day after he stomped out of the house, she looked at me and very innocently, said, "I really know how to push his buttons, don't I?" Yes, she did and she was well aware of it.

Truthfulness is another strength. When you see things in black and white perspective as Kalisha and most people with autism do, truthfulness can occasionally cause problems. It isn't that I want her to lie or not speak truth, but to be aware of other's feelings. A few years ago, I was fitted for hearing aids. Kalisha saw that as a marvelous improvement. We attended a banquet the first day I had them. As soon as we sat down, she announced to the 8 people sitting at the table, "Guess what. Mom got hearing aids today."

Because it would never bother her if someone said something like that about her, she can't imagine why it would bother anyone else. I have written lots of blog posts about her. In the beginning, she would read them before they were published. She no longer wants to. She tells me she doesn't care what I write *about* her. She just wants people to know what it is like to *be* her.

Her nieces and nephews have angrily accused me of always believing Kalisha, when there is a disagreement about a situation that transpired. They're correct. I have never known her to knowingly lie. She even tells on herself. I can't count the times she came home and her first words as she came through the door were, "Know what I did today?" or "Know what happened today?" I would probably never know what happened, but she feels the need to tell on herself. I'm glad she does, although there have been times I wish I didn't have to hear it.

Her friendliness is an asset, also. She has great customer service skills. She never fails to call a salesperson, cashier, waitress or bank teller (anyone wearing a nametag) by their name. She usually asks a question of some sort also. Her ability and willingness to speak to anyone has repercussions sometimes, but for the most part, people respond to her. She has no prejudices; she accepts people as they are. She may not always want to associate with some groups, but she doesn't dislike or disparage them. Kalisha knows a LOT of people; from every culture, race, religion, economic status, age group, gender and sexual and political persuasion. Although she may have some questions or opinions, she respects their right to be. She would like to be 'normal,' as she expresses it, but she accepts herself and her labels. She has always believed if you have a problem with her, it is *your* problem, not *hers*.

Kalisha has a sense of humor, although most of the time, she acts as though she doesn't know what she said was funny. While watching television, *without* my hearing aids, I asked, "What did she just say?" She told me. Then I asked, "Now what did he say?" Kalisha turned to me and calmly said, "I don't know. I couldn't hear him because I was too busy telling you what *she* said." I laughed but then had to explain why that was funny.

She is an encourager. She is my cheerleader when it comes to any new endeavor I tackle. If I have not been writing for a few days, she will ask,

"Have you finished the article you were working on?" or "Did you meet your deadline?" She likes to let people know when I have something published. That can be embarrassing at times, but I'm happy she is proud of my efforts.

Her phone, computer and social media skills have already been chronicled. If our television remote has a problem, I hand it to her. Most of the time, she can remedy the situation. If she can't fix a problem or get a new app installed on her phone, she will call tech support until someone gets an answer for her. She will not hesitate to call any person, company, store, television station or any place she believes will have an answer to her question, whether it is technical or information related. Recently, on Facebook, she saw a picture of Andrew Luck (NFL quarterback) on a box of Lucky Charms cereal. She began searching for that cereal in every store. When I didn't hear about it for a few days, I asked if she had given up her search.

She said, "It's not real. It was Photoshopped." I asked how she knew that for sure.

She replied, "I called General Mills and they told me."

Who calls General Mills? Kalisha, apparently.

Some of her *weaknesses* are behavioral. Her inability to make good decisions concerning money, relationships and use of her time and her stubborn, unyielding stance on some situations fall into the behavioral category.

Other weaknesses are physical and fall into the small motor skill category. Many of these weaknesses have a surprising counterpoint that she is able to accomplish. Some of them don't matter to me, or to her ability to survive in this world. When it is feasible, I have made accommodations; sort of like widening a doorway for someone who uses a wheelchair.

Using a scissors is a skill she has never mastered. When she tries to cut something, it looks as though she chewed it off. She can live without that particular skill.

She can't write cursive; she prints everything. Since the schools are going to eliminate cursive writing, she will fit right in.

She is a notoriously bad speller. If you have seen any texts people send, you know her spelling looks like everyone else's.

Although Kalisha is very strong, you don't want to ask for her help when lifting or moving something. It is a motor-planning skill many special needs individuals don't possess. She can't lift anything heavy more than a few inches off the ground. If she isn't applying for a job with a furniture company, that probably won't matter, either.

She has difficulty putting clothes on hangers and then putting the hangers on a rod. I removed the rod in our hall closet and added hooks. Problem solved.

Buttoning clothing is hard but she has mastered a zipper. She owns nothing with buttons.

She can't buckle a watchband. She buys watches with Velcro bands.

She can tie her shoes, but usually ties them loosely enough so she can push her foot in without untying and re-tying the laces. Do I care? No.

She can't use a blade-style razor to shave her legs. She learned that the hard way, with blood running down her legs. She now has a battery-operated razor.

She is unable to clip her toenails or fingernails. When I'm no longer around to help her, she can pay to get a manicure and pedicure.

Kalisha is able to brush her teeth with no problem but the ability to floss them eludes her. We tried a flosser with a long handle like a toothbrush. She still could not get it in the right position.

She is afraid of using the stove. This has improved since she goes to cooking class, but most of the time, she uses the microwave. Why not? It's possible to make a lot of things in the microwave and survive.

For years, she could never brush through the hair at the nape of her neck. That resulted in a 'rat's nest' close to her scalp that I would sometimes have to cut out. But, she can put her hair in a ponytail and do the 'twist' action with an elastic band around it.

I have to admit Kalisha is lazy and has the speed of a sloth. She has good intentions to clean her room, change her sheets, take the dog for a walk or fix lunch but never quite gets around to it. I take responsibility for making things way too easy for way too long. We are working on this problem.

I make a conscious effort to not dwell on her weaknesses. I help her adapt to them, while I am continually amazed at some of her skills and strengths. I don't believe she is done learning new things or growing in her understanding so we continue to walk this journey together.

Remember not every challenge *can* be overcome and not all *need* to be. It is permissible to adapt certain difficult things to make them easier for our children while still striving to teach them the necessary skills to live independently in the future.

Kalisha's Money

"MOM, I DIDN'T have enough cash to pay for my meal at Burger King."

"Again? So, what did you do this time?"

"I told them I needed that meal, but I only had 3 dollars."

"Why didn't you get just the burger and tell them to skip the fries and drink?"

"I was hungry for the whole meal. But it worked out okay, because the manager came and told the girl to just give it to me."

"Were they busy, Kalisha, with lots of people waiting behind you?"

"Yes."

This was not the first time I had heard this tale. She had done the same thing several other times. I tried to decide if she thought she had found a way to get her meals without spending her money. They always felt sorry for her or wanted her out of the line, so they let her get by with it. We had long discussions about how it was a form of stealing and when businesses lose money they go out of business. She seemed to understand but we are continually working on adding the cost of items and checking that amount against the amount of money she has BEFORE getting in line.

There are many stories concerning Kalisha and money; I'm not sure where to begin.

She informed me one afternoon several years ago, she had purchased something from e-Bay. I was very concerned. I had visions of a '57 Buick showing up in my driveway. Actually, she had purchased several books, not Buicks. Thank you, Lord.

She had also opened a PayPal account to make it easier to purchase things. It wouldn't be necessary to enter her debit card number with each purchase; just use PayPal. How had she learned to do these things? Self-taught. She looks things up online, Googles her questions until she finds a way to accomplish whatever it is she wants to do. It's scary, actually. Just because she knows the mechanics of purchasing, does not mean she has any grasp of money.

Most people are honest. The people who purposely cheated her are in the minority, but it is always a concern. An acquaintance wanted to borrow money from Kalisha. She told them she didn't have her card and therefore no way to get cash from the ATM machine. This person accompanied her to the bank and showed her how to fill out a counter check. She didn't think it was at all unusual; in fact, she told me when she came home because she was proud of learning something new. She also lost $20 that day.

I gave her the debit card when she had her hair cut. A beautician 'helped' by telling her to write $25 on the *tip* line. Kalisha wrote it in. Nice tip, huh?

Those are only a few of the bizarre things that happened with her debit card. You can read about an entire day of someone else spending her money in another chapter. The problem with giving her cash instead of her card was then anyone could talk her out of the money in her purse and it would be so much easier for an unscrupulous cashier to not give her the correct change after a purchase. You may wonder if that isn't true of everyone using cash. I believe people can probably perceive the fact that Kalisha isn't good with money and won't know the difference.

Kalisha has some strange ideas about money. She never wants to break a bill. If she spends only $2 out of a twenty-dollar bill, she will tell me her purchase cost twenty dollars, because that was the amount she had to give the cashier. The $18 change she received doesn't count in her head. If I borrow a ten-dollar bill from her, I can't pay her back with 2 five-dollar bills or a five and 5 ones. She needs to be repaid in the same form she loaned.

She never uses any coins to pay for a purchase, only bills, until recently. She asked me to take her to the grocery for a particular item she wanted. I waited in the car. She didn't come out for a long time, so I went in looking for her. She was standing at a self-checkout, inserting 8 dollars' worth of change, one coin at a time. I knew she would have a receipt about 4-feet long.

Kalisha is obviously very good at the techie part of buying and selling. She knows how to check her bank balances using her phone. She knows how to transfer funds from her savings account to her checking account using her computer or phone. But she still can't make change and doesn't know if she is getting the correct change.

Kalisha doesn't actually buy much, as some 'shoppers' do. When she gets it in her head that she wants something specific, she can't reason with herself that it may be too expensive or she needs to wait until the next month or perhaps she doesn't need it at all.

Each year, there is a huge Vera Bradley outlet sale in our city. Even though Kalisha has mostly Colts purses, she finds a new Vera Bradley pattern she likes online, before the sale and has to have a couple pieces of it. I always accompany her to the sale. If I didn't I'm not sure how much she would spend. She would purchase one of every item in the pattern she likes.

When she has her mind set on something, she is like a dog with a bone. Following is a sample of her tenacity and her intelligence when she wanted a new phone. It gets complicated. Follow closely:

Kalisha checked her phone status with Verizon on the internet. She found that she was due for an 'upgrade' on July 1st.

Kalisha is a phone junkie. She loves her phone, takes good care of it and uses it more than her computer. It goes everywhere with her.

I used to get upset when she always wanted the next great phone, but

I have backed off. She never buys jewelry, seldom buys makeup, and only a few new clothes. Her phone is her 'hot button.'

She wanted to get on the bus and go to Verizon the next day. It was still June. Her upgrade wasn't until July.

This is our conversation for the next few hours:

"Kalisha, you can't buy it until your upgrade date. The phone you want will cost you $200 if you wait. Before that date, it will cost you full price, which is about $600. Do you have $600 dollars?"

"No, but I think I can get the phone early; before my upgrade date."

"The only way you can get it *anytime* is if you find a buyer for the 4S phone you have now."

Later....

"Hey, Mom, I called Verizon and they will give me $140 for my 4S."

"Okay. Then your new phone would only be $60. You can probably do that."

Later...

"Mom, I found a lady on Craigslist who wants to buy an I-phone 4S and she will pay $180 for it."

"Great. Did you tell her she can't have it until the 1st of July?"

"No. But I will."

"Hey, Mom, I found an I-phone 5 on Craigslist and he only wants $150.00 for it. He says it is new and still in the package."

"If it's still in the package, it is probably hot."

"What does that mean? It's stolen?"

"Yes. Possibly."

Later....

"I called Verizon and they will give me $200 for the I-phone 5, so if I get on the bus, meet the lady and sell her mine for $140, then add $10 to it and buy the I-phone 5 from the guy for $150 and then sell that to Verizon for $200, my new phone will be free, won't it?"

(This is the kid who can't count money and can't get the right change for things)

"Oh my gosh, Kalisha. I don't know if it will be free or not. You lost me somewhere along the line. Regardless, you still can't upgrade until July 1st and you told me the Iphone 5 he has for sale is on a Sprint network. I don't know if they can switch it to Verizon."

"I'll call and find out."

"I'm sure you will."

"No, they can't switch networks but they will still give me $200 for it, so can I go buy his phone?"

"No. Where are you going to get the $150 for his phone?"

"I don't know, but he's waiting for me to let him know."

Later...

"I found another one on Craigslist and he will sell it for $140.00. That's cheaper, right? And then I can still sell it to Verizon."

"What happened to the woman who wanted to buy yours?"

"She didn't want to wait until July 1st."

"Maybe she is related to you, Kalisha."

Puzzled..."Why?"

Finally, I said, "Here's the deal. Stop trying to buy and sell today. Just wait and you can sell your phone to Verizon for $140 and your new one will cost you $60."

Have we come full circle in this conversation yet? Wait..it gets better.

"Okay. I am getting on the bus, going to Verizon and maybe they will sell it to me. Can you loan me the $60 until the 3rd of July, just in case?"

I loaned her $60 cash.

"Good idea. Go." I *knew* they were not going to sell it early.

My phone rings. "Mom what is the password on the account?"

"Why do you need it?"

"Just so they can look up my date and everything."

I gave it to her, knowing she did not have her debit card with her. Otherwise she might have paid the full $600 for it since she wanted it that day.

My phone rings again. "Hi Kalisha. Did they sell you the phone early?"

"No. They said they couldn't. But when I left the store, I called customer service and told them how much I wanted that phone and the lady said since I am a loyal Verizon customer, she would do it. My phone will be delivered on Wednesday and then I can take my 4S in and sell it to them. Isn't that cool?"

She came in the door, smiling from ear to ear and handed me a slip of paper. "Oh yeah, since they are going to put the price of the phone on the bill, I stopped at the bank and put your $60 back into your checking account because I knew you would need it."

"Do you know the number of my checking account???" I asked, rather incredulously. I was pretty sure my bank would not let anyone deposit money to someone's account unless they knew the number.

"No, but they let me do it anyway."

All the tellers at our bank know Kalisha and although they would not have let her *withdraw* any funds from my account, they did allow her to *deposit* money.

Kalisha also suffers from a severe form of 'buyer's remorse.' Many times she purchases things, then processes her actions on the way home. By the time she is entering the house, her first words are, "I'm going to take it back. I have the receipt."

She is generous to a fault. She will, and has, helped her nieces and nephews when they needed to borrow a few dollars. She likes to buy things for people she loves and she gives a bit to every person standing on a street corner holding a sign.

She pays a portion of the household expenses and her own cell phone bill. Her monthly check is directly deposited into her account and I transfer the amount she owes for living expenses to my account. She doesn't have to be responsible for that, but if she wants to be independent and live on her own some day; I should have her 'hand' me the cash or write a check for her expenses. We have tried various methods of money management and recently returned to the 'envelope system.' She has an envelope for each monthly expense. Like the rest of the human race, if one envelope is empty, she sees no reason to not borrow from another one.

Her concept of money vacillates between brilliant as in her negotiating skills, to very childlike when she is at Burger King with only a few dollars. She does not stop to add the price of her items before ordering or checking out. She doesn't think ahead at all. What will she do if she doesn't have enough money? That thought doesn't even enter her mind until it is too late.

Literal Thinking

There was a time when I worked in a residential cleaning business. One of the houses we cleaned had a huge room in the lower level with a black and white checkerboard- patterned floor. It was a distinct pattern; no gray, no blurring, absolute straight black and white lines. When I cleaned that floor, I always thought of Kalisha and how she lives in a straight-lined, no gray areas, black and white world. It is hard for us to imagine because we encounter gray areas and blurred lines all the time and don't even realize it.

I'm not referencing the gray areas between right and wrong, although for many people, there are a lot of those. I am referring to the areas of joking, saying things kiddingly, being facetious, using double-meanings, hidden humor, odd sayings, inside jokes, euphemisms or idioms. I became aware just how often we use language like this after Kalisha was born.

Black and white thinking, also known as literal thinking is a trait that is common to nearly all individuals on the autism and Asperger's spectrum.

There are times when she will act as though she understands, but if I question her, she will admit she doesn't. When she was very young, if I said it was raining cats and dogs, she might have looked outside to see if it really was. As she matured, she knew there were no cats and dogs falling from the sky, but she still wouldn't know what I meant. If I explained it meant it was raining really hard, she would ask, "Why don't you just say it's raining hard?" Good point.

Trying to explain empathy or how someone else might feel, I said, "Put yourself in her shoes."

That didn't compute at all. How was she going to put herself in someone else's shoes?

We were at an IEP meeting. When it concluded, one teacher stated he had better get home because his wife kept him on a short chain, around his leg. I noticed Kalisha immediately looking at his legs. I tried explaining that one on the way home.

Last week she told me, "I think it's going to snow."

I answered with, "I can hardly wait for that!" She gave me a very strange look.

I said, "I'm just being facetious." Another quizzical look.

Then I asked, "Do you know what that means?"

"No."

Do you know how difficult it is to define facetious? I should have told her I was kidding. She knows what that means, but doesn't really understand why anyone is 'kidding.' I can't count how many times I ask, "Do you know what that word means?" or "Do you understand why that was funny?" It's a great teaching tool, but sometimes *I* begin to wonder why we say things that mean the opposite of what we really mean. I think Kalisha's way might be best. Say what you mean.

When Kalisha was young, she would be excited about a visit we were going to make to a friend's home. As soon as we arrived, she would invariably ask, "When are we leaving?" This always annoyed me until the light dawned and I figured out she didn't want to leave, she wanted to know *when* we were leaving. She is still that way today. Whether it is a vacation, a visit or a trip to the grocery, she is uncomfortable until she knows when we are leaving home, how long we will be there and when we will return. She isn't rigid in abiding to the times, thank goodness, but still likes to have a time frame.

She hates it when I answer her questions with, "I'll think about it." or "We'll have to wait and see." or "Maybe." She likes definitive answers and will always give one. I have never heard Kalisha say 'maybe.'

While Kalisha does not always fit the stereotypical description of many people with autism, there are some traits that are definitely on that spectrum. Some people believe individuals on the spectrum have no emotions. That is not true. They have emotions; they do not show emotion and when they do, it is often inappropriate. Except for times of extreme circumstances, (crying when her little dog was killed or screaming with excitement when the Colts won the Super Bowl) Kalisha does not show much emotion. Sadness, anger, disappointment or happiness can all look the same. There were many times when her facial expressions were totally inappropriate for the situation. For instance, she might ask someone who recently lost their husband, "So, do you miss Ernie since he died?" That question is appropriate, but she would ask it with a big smile on her face.

To help overcome that, we practiced with pretend conversations. Even that was a struggle because pretending is not something that comes naturally to Kalisha. I might say, "Okay. Let's pretend I am crying because I just fell down and skinned my knee. What would you say to me?" She would look at my knee and I knew what she was thinking: I didn't have a hurt knee, why should she say anything to me?

She likes to own Build-a-Bear stuffed animals and American Girl dolls but she never plays with them. If she is having a bad day, she may hold one of them for comfort, but she isn't able to 'talk' to them.

Imagining things is foreign to her. Even though she knows the programs on television and scenes in movies are not real, she will occasionally question, "They didn't really get hurt, right?"

She likes the mascots for the sports teams she watches. I know that she understands there are people inside the costumes and still there must be a bit of confusion in her brain. Every once in a while, she needs to reassure herself the mascots aren't real. She will ask me just to reaffirm that fact.

When we went to Disney World, she was pushed to her limits on what was real and what wasn't. When she saw Barney, she jumped on the walkway with him and gave him a big hug. Cinderella came to our table when we ate in the castle. I know there were hundreds of children there who believed they were seeing the real Cinderella. The difference was they were quite young and Kalisha was 15.

Enjoying Cinderella

Spectator Sports

WHEN IT COMES to sports, Kalisha has been a spectator most of her life. When she was only a few weeks old, I took her to watch her sister, Kendra, play elementary school basketball. That was just the beginning. Not only did her siblings play organized sports, but then her nieces and nephews played. She has probably logged more 'bleacher hours' than anyone I know. Between the 4 families, she has attended innumerable baseball, basketball, volleyball, football and soccer games, skateboarding events and wrestling matches. She never complained and was always eager to go.

She did play softball on a special needs team for several summers. She liked it, but didn't feel like she fit in there. What she so badly wanted was to play on a REAL team as she referred to regulation teams. That, of course, never happened.

Kalisha's siblings and their spouses are all NFL football fans, each having their own favorite team. Kalisha never paid much attention to football until she was in high school. I'm not sure if she got tired of everyone else having a team to cheer for or if she suddenly made that age leap of liking football.

Photo provided by Frederick's Photography—Huntington, Indiana

Playing softball on a 'special needs' team

Either way, she chose the Indianapolis Colts as her team and they have never had a more loyal fan. She did her research as she tends to do with anything she likes. She even wrote a report on Johnny Unitas, a quarterback for the Colts from the 1950s to the 1970s, when they were the Baltimore Colts. When I asked why she wrote a report about him, she replied, "Because he was important to the team and I want to know all about the Colts."

By the time she became a fan, Peyton Manning was quarterback and they were obviously the Indianapolis Colts. In the beginning, as we watched each game, I thought she was just watching and cheering when there was a touchdown. I soon learned she knew more about the game than I ever imagined was possible for her. She understood the downs, the penalties, the yardage, kickoffs and all the other jargon associated with football. I haven't quite figured out what it is about the game that makes it easy for her to comprehend. Possibly the fact that the rules are constant and there aren't too many variables. Whatever it is, she is hooked.

Kalisha is a true Colts fan

She has nearly every item produced that has a Colts horseshoe on it. A brief list would include shirts, shoes, socks, sweatshirts, coats, scarves, gloves, summer and winter hats, bookmarks, clocks, calendars, cups, jewelry, fingernail polish, pillows, bedspread, blankets, rug, and an entire decorated bedroom, with white and blue walls. She has a Fathead (removable life-size decal) of a favorite player on one wall.

A reporter and photographer from the local newspaper came to interview her and take pictures of her in her Colts bedroom. The ½ page color article was in the newspaper on Super Bowl Sunday. It was a big deal. She loved it. After that article appeared in the paper, several nice people who were season ticket holders sent her their tickets for preseason games they were unable to attend.

When Tony Dungy came to town to sign the book he wrote, we stood in line for hours but weren't able to get his autograph. She sent her copy of his book with return postage and explained how she had waited. He graciously signed her book and sent it back.

Last year when the new coach, Chuck Pagano, was diagnosed with leukemia, she earnestly prayed for his recovery. One day, she received a package in the mail with rubber bracelets in it. I questioned her and she told me they were sent to her by Coach Pagano's sister.

"How do you know Chuck Pagano's sister?" I asked.

"We are friends on Facebook and we e-mail back and forth. I told her I would hand out the bracelets for her and she sent them."

Sometimes I can't think of any response and my mouth just hangs open.

Occasionally, a few cheerleaders, players, and Blue, the team mascot, make an appearance at a local mall or other venue. We always have to go so she can talk to them, get their autographs and have a picture taken. When I see her talking to the players, I assume she is discussing plays with them. Probably not, but her intensity makes it look like she is.

When Peyton Manning was not re-signed by the Colts, she just about came unglued. She was very sad and upset about it, but accepted Andrew Luck as the new quarterback and gave him her support, 100 percent. She still loves Peyton and watches all of the Denver Bronco games, but when I asked who she was going to cheer for when the Broncos played the Colts, she looked at me like that was the dumbest question she ever heard.

"Well, I'll cheer for the Colts. That's my team." And so it is.

We drove to Anderson, IN, for training camp a few years ago. She got autographs from some of the players. This year we returned. When we arrived she bought a leather football just for autographs. The players practice for several hours and then some of them come to the fence to sign autographs.

To begin with, it rained like it was the monsoon season. We were soaked to the skin. Kalisha was afraid to sit on the bleachers with me for fear she wouldn't get back to the fence when it was time for autographs. This girl, who does not do well standing for long periods of time, stood at the fence for nearly 2 hours with her football.

The fence was as long as the field and various players came to different sections of it. As I watched, Andrew Luck was headed directly for the section where she was standing.

Waiting for an autograph

"Oh please, God," I prayed. "Please let him sign her football." The crush of people at the fence was unbelievable. They were 6 deep reaching out to the players. She stood her ground and yes, he did sign her football.

Andrew Luck's autograph

Thank you, Lord. She managed to get several other signatures that day, also. On the way home, we discussed idol worship and the fact the players are just men who happen to be very good at what they do. She understood completely.

The next day she told me to go to the Colts' website. There were 85 pictures from the previous day's practice. Only 3 of the 85 were of the fans and yes, she was in one of those 3, holding her football out to Andrew Luck. How cool was that? Very cool.

During the summer, she is just as ardent a fan of the local minor league baseball team and their mascot, Johnny. The team is named the TinCaps after Johnny Appleseed who is buried in a park in our city. The folklore says he wore his cooking pot on his head while wandering the countryside starting apple orchards; hence, the TinCaps. Kalisha attends every game she can and always has her picture taken with Johnny.

Again, she researched John Chapman, his real name. She read every book about him the library had available and memorized all the facts about his life.

The team promotion for a game we attended was to give away the night's team jerseys to 16 lucky fans, after the game. Everyone filled out their entry. Of the 8000 fans there, guess who won one of the jerseys? Kalisha, of course. It was the pitcher's jersey. She had him sign it and had her picture taken with him.

She has to have her picture taken with Johnny, the mascot, at every game she attends. She is, literally, willing to climb over railings or people to get to the place where he is, with her phone in hand so an employee can take the picture. Occasionally, I attend a game with her. As we walk along the stadium's corridor and the Tincap employees we see, greet her by name, saying, "Hi Kalisha," it tells me she has definitely made a name for herself at the stadium. I'm never sure if that is a good thing or not but I prefer to think it is.

Kalisha doesn't own many shirts that don't have either Colts or TinCaps logos on them. She wears them everywhere; shopping, church, volunteering, etc. I used to waste my breath trying to convince her to wear something else. However, it was a battle I wasn't willing to fight. The shirts are always clean and neat. I no longer hassle her about it.

Many sports teams have loyal and demonstrative fans. In that regard, Kalisha is like thousands of others. However, her interest borders on the obsessive and fanatic. (Not the dangerous kind) She almost regards the mascots as real people. She knows there are people inside the costumes, but she talks about Blue and Johnny as if *they* were real. Every once in a while, we go over the fact they are just people dressed in costumes.

Her 30th birthday is in February of 2014. She is planning a birthday party to end all birthday parties. She is trying to reserve Blue, the Colts' mascot and Johnny, the TinCaps' mascot for her party. We have reserved the church reception room to hold all the guests she will invite. After discussing it with me, she has called and made these arrangements herself. She is saving her money to pay for it.

When I think about her party plans, I am reminded of the 2 differing ages and abilities within Kalisha. On the one end of the spectrum is the fact she wants the 2 mascots at her party. On the other end is her ability to find the websites, numbers, prices, contact people and make all of these arrangements herself.

After telling several people this party will be a 'blow-out," she turned to me and asked, "What is a blow-out, anyway?"

Sighs, Thighs and Exercise

WEIGHT HAS ALWAYS been a concern since Kalisha hit puberty. There are several reasons for this problem, none of which are very scientific.

#1: She really, really likes fast food
#2: She really, really does not like to exercise
#3: The propensity for many special needs individuals to be overweight (once again, I have no scientific data to support this; just my observations)
#4: She has me for a mother, who doesn't set the best example in the exercise department.

Add those up and you have an overweight young woman. Sigh.

She was not a chubby baby; just average. She wasn't a chubby little kid; in fact she could have been classified as thin. But when she hit puberty (really early) things went downhill or *uphill*, on the scale.

It's not like we haven't tried several times and several different ideas. When we lived on the farm, she rode her bike every day and ran around with the dogs, helped with chores and played in the pasture with the goats. We also had a treadmill she liked to use nearly every morning. When we moved to town, we were fortunate enough to be in an apartment complex with an exercise room. Needless to say, she didn't use it nearly as much as she had at home, where she could jump on it anytime she wanted without going outside. She didn't want to ride her bike in the complex or on the road (I wasn't wild about her doing that either) and she didn't like the pool.

We decided, after investigating the benefits, to join Curves. It seemed perfect; low impact exercises, easy-to-use machines and using all the core muscles. We each bought a year's membership, with high hopes. It was a really expensive adventure since we only went 4 times in a year. It wasn't Curves fault; we just didn't have the desire to go. It was never the right time of day, it was too cold, too hot or we were too tired. One excuse is as good as another when you don't want to do something. Sigh.

We also tried The Atkins Diet. Kalisha's sister, Kari, lost many pounds and inches following this way of eating. One of the terms she would use when talking about it was how she would 'balance' some particular food with another one. Kalisha liked that and would use it often. The problem was her balancing wasn't always exactly right. After eating a cupcake, she would say, "It's okay. I'll just balance this with an apple." Needless to say, that didn't work so well.

We knew someone who was having great success with Weight Watchers. Okay, we could do this. We didn't have to go to meetings, we had the books with all the points listed for nearly every food on the planet. We did okay for a while, but Kalisha got tired of looking up various foods and writing down the points, then adding them up for the day. So-o-o Weight Watchers bit the dust, too.

Kalisha wanted to join the YWCA. She had a friend who rode the bus with her and she went to the 'Y' all the time. She purchased a membership. (We aren't fast learners) The friend didn't go as much as she said she did and the 'Y' that Kalisha liked the best was in another part of town. This wouldn't have been a problem if the bus route didn't stop a mile from the facility. By the time she walked there, she was too tired to exercise. Another waste of money.

Her occupational therapist brought her Wii from home and they exercised with the dance program, but since we didn't own a Wii, she was limited in how much she could use it. She has 3 VHS tapes of Richard Simmons' "Sweatin' To the Oldies." She did these faithfully for quite a while. She had to use them in the basement because I was afraid she would go through the wood floor in the living room. Sigh

Using the Wii for exercise

She also watched a commercial for the Special K foods and drinks. She purchased some, liked the bars and cereal but the drinks were not her cup of tea. I think we still have a few bottles but they expired a long time ago.

Kalisha is not 'flabby' fat. She is built like the proverbial *brick outhouse.* You cannot grab a pinch of skin anywhere on her legs, thighs or derriere. She is solid.

She hates her big breasts, her arms, midriff and belly. She refuses to wear anything but a size 3X shirt, so it will hang over her waist and hide her belly. She could wear an XL or 2X quite well, but she is very self-conscious about how it looks. She almost had apoplexy last summer when she volunteered at the zoo and had to tuck her shirt into the waistband of her shorts. She wants to wear zip-up jeans like all the other girls, but has to buy jeans with elastic waists to be comfortable.

She had breast reduction surgery several years ago, but of course, when she gained weight, the first place it went was back to her breasts.

She knows all the benefits of losing weight. She will, in all probability, inherit bad knees. Losing some weight would decrease her chances of needing knee replacement surgery. Her father has slight diabetes; she doesn't want that, either. She has sleep apnea, which would decrease if she lost weight.

Kalisha is well aware of these benefits and can recite them, verbatim, for you, but that Big Mac calls her name every time she thinks about it. Sigh.

She is embarking on a new journey with Weight Watchers. They now have an app for her phone that makes it so much easier. She can scan a bar code on any product and immediately know how many points and what serving size. Since she is such a phone junkie, this is right up her alley. She paid for 3 months' membership. I know, I know...at least it's not a year this time. Another sigh......

Clothing Choices

KALISHA WAS ALWAYS dressed in matching, color-coordinated outfits when she was young. When my other 4 children were little, I would occasionally allow them to dress themselves when they insisted, "I can do it myself."

As all parents know, that usually results in mismatches, shirts buttoned unevenly and occasionally, clothing on backwards. I never felt I could allow Kalisha that privilege. I thought she had enough things going against her, as far as the other children were concerned, and I didn't want to add one more thing they could tease her about. In retrospect, I don't know if that was wise or not. But I do know she received an award for 'The Best Dressed Student' when she was in pre-school. I was happy; it meant nothing to Kalisha.

Clothes were not important to her then and never have been, unless it involves something she does *not* want to wear. She was in kindergarten when I bought her a pair of green, summer canvas shoes. She didn't like them when I brought them home and usually refused to wear them. I (foolishly) insisted she put them on for school one morning. They matched her shirt color, don't you know?

She got on the bus grumbling about those shoes. An hour later, I received a call from the principal asking me to pick her up because she hit another child. I could hardly believe that. When she got in the car, I questioned her about it.

"Well," she said, "I knew Mr. Crews would send me home if I hit somebody."

The light was beginning to dawn.... "And you wanted to come home for what?"

She looked down at her green shoes and said, "So I could change my shoes."

I should have realized then she had very definite ideas about what she liked or what was comfortable and what was not.

She didn't like skirts, turtlenecks, sweaters, leotards (what little girl does?), dressy shoes, capri pants or a host of other things. The term, *sensory issues*, was not in my vocabulary at that time but I did have enough sense to realize she wasn't just being obstinate; they really did bother her.

Kalisha was advised by a job coach to buy some dressier clothes for interviews. We went shopping for nice slacks; plain colors, elastic waistbands. Then we looked for a few coordinating shirts to wear with them. These were not anything particularly dressy; just casual clothes. She agreed to a few, tried them on and they were approved. They never left the hangers in her closet. Several years later, she sold them at a garage sale.

She knows what she likes and what she is comfortable wearing. She likes jeans, T-shirts, and anything with the Indianapolis Colts' logo on it. During football season, she wears nothing but Colts gear. She likes to tell people that she would wear Colts underwear too, but the only kind they sell is bikinis and she won't wear them.

She had several fleece pants and shirts that bear Colts designs, also. She wore them to church quite often. One Sunday she was asked by a young kid why she was wearing her pajamas to church. She told him in no uncertain terms they were *not* pajamas.

Her friend purchased some lightweight pants and tops with Disney designs on them for summer sleepwear. Of course, Kalisha wanted some just like them. The only difference was her friend wore hers as pajamas and Kalisha wore hers as street clothes.

Colts shoes

A good friend of ours called to ask if Kalisha could be her husband's 'date' for the night. She had to work late and thought perhaps Kalisha would like to accompany him to a baseball game at our local minor league stadium. Kalisha was excited to go and chose to wear one of the Disney outfits. I learned later it was his company's annual business outing; food, prizes, box seats and all. I wondered if any of those 'important' people were wondering why Kalisha was wearing something that looked vaguely like pajamas.

In Kalisha's senior year in high school, she wanted to go to the prom. Now, came the fun part…looking for a dress. One that Kalisha was comfortable wearing, looked good and didn't cost a million dollars because I knew it would be worn only once.

I tried steering her to the 'prom dress' department, but she was definitely not interested in anything glittery, short, sleeveless or *swishy*. We ended up in what I thought was the 'old lady dresses' but she did find one she liked. Shoes were another matter. I drew the line at sneakers with a long dress. She eventually agreed to wear a pair of mine with no heels. Whew! She was ready to go.

She continues to have issues with clothes. During the summer, she got a volunteer job at our local children's zoo. They require a shirt and hat with the zoo's logo on it. You can buy your own khaki shorts. All was well until she realized she had to tuck her shirt into her shorts. She didn't like the way it made her belly look and she complained about it every time she went. She made it through the season, but needless to say, she is not volunteering there again. Is anyone interested in khaki shorts and a bright red polo?

Kalisha is very self-conscious of her large breasts. Therefore, she will not wear any shirt that isn't a size 3X. She could actually wear an XL but refuses. She won a shirt at a function and after looking at the size, she went to customer service and asked for a larger one. They were very accommodating.

I have learned to not *sweat the small stuff* when it comes to clothing. It took me a while to get to that point, but if I was honest, it was because I was worried about people's perception of *me* as a parent, as well as their thoughts about Kalisha.

She is always clean and tidy, she doesn't wear anything stained or wrinkled. So, as long as she is comfortable, why do I care?

I Was Invited To the Dance

As I STATED in the introduction, I was once told I didn't have to attend every power struggle to which I was invited. That is such wonderful, practical, liberating advice, which I try very hard to follow. There are times, however, when I fail miserably.

I start many conversations by offering Kalisha a few reasons why something isn't possible but when I see she is in Kalisha Mode, I have learned to back off and refuse to argue about it any longer because further talking is pointless. HOWEVER, sometimes I accept the invitation to the *dance of the power struggle* and we go 'round and 'round, doing the 2-step.

Recently, I was given an invitation and although I tried not to attend, eventually I did walk through that door.

The party started when my granddaughter and her girlfriend purchased 2 boxes of the ready-to-bake Disney cookies. One box with a 'Cars' imprint in the middle and the other had a Minnie Mouse imprint. They burned at least one, possibly two, pans of cookies. I saw the cremated remains in the wastebasket when I dumped the coffee grounds in the trash in the morning.

Boxes of cookies Kalisha HAD to have

When Kalisha awoke and saw those Disney boxes and cookies, she was immediately going to the store to purchase some of the same boxes of cookies. Here is where I should have ignored the invitation, but of course, I didn't. I told her she could eat one of the cookies the girls had left on the table, but she didn't need to buy more. That wasn't good enough. *She wanted her own boxes of cookies to bake.* I tried reasoning: too expensive, too many calories, I wasn't going to the store. I believe it was at this point she said she was going to eat the burned ones that were in the trash.

Now I wasn't just *attending* the party, I had my ball gown and slippers on and we were going to dance for a while.

I mentioned the fact they were covered in coffee grounds. She stated she didn't care and was going to eat them, anyway. I also quoted a few bible verses about envy. That certainly didn't make any difference.

I should mention that she never screams, yells or has a tantrum. She just keeps repeating what she is going to do and nothing I say will budge her or change her mind.

After telling me she was going to dig them out of the trash, I took her phone and sent her to her room. That action is the equivalent of the scene in the movies where someone slaps the hysterical person. She stayed in her room for a few hours, had a nap and came down saying she was sorry. She still wanted to buy the cookies sometime, but she wasn't "locked in" as she had been.

In retrospect, I could have refused the invitation by telling her to dust the coffee grounds off the burned cookies and go right ahead and eat them. I wonder if she would have learned anything by eating burned cookies.

The same one-mindedness I am complaining about has stood her in good stead at various times in her life. She learned to walk simply by getting up and trying again every time she fell down. I realize the same is true of every child learning to walk, but Kalisha fell down and got back up a zillion more times than others.

She wanted to ride a bicycle, although she had never mastered a tricycle. It took 3 years for her to learn to ride the 2-wheeler, but she did it. The fact she could only work on one action at a time caused her lots of problems. When she was concentrating on pedaling, she couldn't steer and when she was steering, her feet would come off the pedals because she would lose her concentration. She would have given up, but all her nieces and nephews were coming to the farm for a 4th of July camping weekend. We had a long driveway and they were all planning on bringing their bikes.

Kalisha started practicing in earnest, on Wednesday. She spent the next 3 days struggling up and down the driveway. By the time everyone arrived on Friday evening, she could ride with them. Not as fast, certainly, but she could ride.

I can hear you saying, 'Just tell her no when she is in Kalisha Mode. How hard can that be?' It is much more difficult than you can imagine. I do start with logic and firm resolve, but at some point, I get tired and I give up. Not always, but occasionally.

I believe this trait, whatever you choose to call it, will be used to her advantage again in her lifetime. I don't know when or where at this point, but I'm absolutely certain it will be. I believe that with all my heart because I know God would want her to use it for good and not just to drive me crazy.

Learning From Pets

KALISHA HAS ALWAYS been comfortable around animals of all kinds. That only stands to reason since she was in the barn in her 'baby carrier' when she was barely 2 weeks old. At the time she was born, we had a goat dairy with many goats, a Great Dane named Marmy, 2 house cats and innumerable barn cats. These were joined by a few chickens, calves, rabbits and pigs.

Napping on Marmy

Marmy adopted Kalisha; watching out for her and staying near any time she was outside. If she was in her stroller while I was mowing the yard, Marmy would position herself between Kalisha and the mower. As I came around the other side of the yard, she would move to the opposite side of the stroller. Marmy allowed Kalisha to take naps using her body as a cushion. She was the original body pillow.

The farm provided many life-lesson opportunities. Because she was nearly always in the barn with me, she learned about necessary daily chores like feeding, watering, giving shots, cleaning stalls and milking.

Kalisha and the goats

One of my first indications we were dealing with autism was due to Kalisha's reaction when I cleaned the automatic milking machines. The glass pipes overhead in the milk room carried the milk slowly to the bulk tank, but when I rinsed the system after milking, the water flowed through the pipes at a rapid pace. Kalisha would become mesmerized by that movement and flap her arms while never taking her eyes off the pipes. I had read enough to know that was not a normal reaction but was sometimes indicative of autism. This was the scenario I nearly always used when describing Kalisha's actions to a new doctor or psychologist.

Helping with the milking

She learned health procedures by observing me when I gave shots or took temperatures. Being the consummate imitator, she wanted to do the same. I heard a cat yowling and found Kalisha holding it by the tail with its back feet off the ground, while trying to insert a very tiny twig to take the cat's temperature; rectally, of course.

She learned some *birds and bees* lessons during breeding season and definitely at birthing time. A large goat named Megan was trying valiantly to deliver her kid (baby goat) while Kalisha was encouraging her by playing midwife. She would say soothing words in Megan's ear and then run to the other end, lift her tail and shout, "Push, Megan, push."

Kalisha learned to walk at a goat show in Ohio. We were there for several days showing our goats when she took tentative steps down the long aisle of the goat barn. The other exhibitors, who were like family to Kalisha, were encouraging and coaxing her to walk from one to another.

Learning to walk in the goat barn

At that time in her life, her extended family included our veterinarian, about 50 goat owners and 200 goats.

I credit Kalisha's being comfortable with people, in part to the early years on the farm. Because of the goat business, she met people of all nationalities: Jewish, Indian, African-American and Hispanic people who came to purchase meat goats. She met the Minister of Agriculture from Taiwan and his interpreter when it was time for exporting. She got to meet nearly every kid in the 4-H program in our county because they all brought their goats to me to tattoo, disbud and castrate.

When I judged a 4-H goat show, she went along and sat on the bleachers. When we showed in open shows, she took a young goat in the ring as soon as she was old enough to hang on to it. When she could enroll in 4-H, she showed many goats at the county fair and won trophies. Did she take care of her 4-H animals all by herself? No. I would have her try to do the trimming and clipping necessary for showing, but her motor skills were not the best for that. She would start the process and I would finish.

Kalisha usually named her pets after Disney characters. The 2 house cats were named Mrs. Potts and Juliet from Beauty and the Beast. She owned a cockatiel she named KT, for King Triton from The Little Mermaid. I wasn't too fond of him, but she loved him. Occasionally, he would sit on her head while she ate her breakfast. She was the only one who could coax him to 'talk.'

We inherited another cat from Kalisha's sister when she moved to Texas. He was a large, beautiful black and white boy named Shadrack. He is still with us today, although he is now 15 years old. He sleeps with Kalisha every night, usually curled around the top of her head.

Marmy was hit by a car and we were all devastated. Kalisha talked out her grief. There were no tears, but lots of talking about Marmy. We had another Great Dane named Shasta and a Cocker Spaniel named Fritz. The two of them and Kalisha were constant companions as they traveled the yard and fields as a threesome, but none of them ever had her heart like Marmy did. Kalisha learned lessons about death also. Shasta had to be put to sleep after a hip injury left her unable to walk or move. Kalisha and I held her head in our laps as the vet administered the injection that freed her from her pain. Several weeks later, Kalisha found Fritz 'asleep' on the front porch. We decided he died of a broken heart because he missed Shasta so much. All of these experiences were instrumental in teaching life lessons to Kalisha; good lessons and sad lessons.

Kalisha watched the movie, Shiloh about 100 times. After our move from the country to the city, she really wanted a dog and of course, she wanted a beagle, just like Shiloh. We found one in the newspaper. Her name was Molly. She came with a crate, bowls, food, collar, everything. It should have been a warning to me when the owner had baby gates in all doorways of his home. Molly was a *runner*. Any time the door opened even a crack, she was out and gone. She was also an *eater*, meaning she would eat anything that didn't eat her first. They say chocolate will kill a dog, but Molly ate an entire box of valentine candy Kalisha received and it didn't even phase her stomach. She also ate a box of crayons. The only effect it had on her was Kalisha came in to tell me she was finding piles of 'rainbow poop' in the yard. We could not keep Molly. We found a home for her with someone who would give her the attention she needed and they had a fenced yard. Everyone involved, including Molly, was much happier. As much as Kalisha wanted her, she did not protest when we gave her away. She was tired of chasing her too.

A few years after that, she bought a Chihuahua named Trixie.

Trixie

This little dog was perfect for Kalisha and they truly loved each other. Kalisha took her for walks and was responsible for her daily needs. Trixie seldom went in the car with us, but I decided to treat her and take her with me to a garage sale. She got past me when I opened the car door and was immediately struck and killed.

When Kalisha came home and I told her, she went through the 7 stages of grief in 5 minutes. She cried, she screamed, she blamed me, she hated me, she sobbed, she denied it and said it couldn't be true. I held her close and we cried together.

I thanked God Trixie was not mangled or bloodied in any way. She looked as though she was asleep. Kalisha helped me bury her and mark her grave in our back yard. That was the most emotion I had ever seen in Kalisha. She asked me to re-enact the entire scenario. I drove to the same spot, turned the car around as I had earlier and stopped where it happened. I believe she needed to experience the reenactment for closure.

She needed to fill the hole in her heart, so several months later, she adopted a dog from the shelter. His name was Iggy. She also adopted a kitten from the shelter, and named her Tabby. Our menagerie now consists of Iggy, Tabby and of course, Shadrack.

To indicate Kalisha is totally responsible for her pets' care would be a lie. She is able to feed and water, brush and go for walks. Does she always want to? No. Do I help her out occasionally? Yes. I clean the litter box, but she has stated several times she needs to learn if she is ever going to live by herself and be able to take Tabby with her.

I allow Kalisha to have pets for several reasons. The daily care teaches responsibility, but it also gives her someone to talk to when she is sad, angry, frustrated with me or with life in general. The pets never judge her motives or try to teach her something or comment on her behavior. They don't care if she hasn't showered or has drool marks on her face when she wakes in the morning. They offer unlimited and unqualified acceptance, which is something a special needs individual doesn't receive too often from humans.

Puberty, Sex and All That Stuff

It seems unfortunate to me that although Kalisha's mind and emotions didn't develop normally for her chronological age, her body did. I wasn't sure how the whole menstruation scene would play out, but I did know I couldn't wait too long to tackle the explanations. If she were true to our 'family form' she would start having her periods at a young age.

I purchased a book with fairly large but simple pictures of male and female reproductive organs, the entire growth progress of a baby in the womb and the subsequent birth. I adapted the text to her level of understanding but she really wasn't interested in knowing all that *stuff.*

Living on a farm was an immense help. I realize not everyone lives on a farm, but for me, it provided some context when talking to her. She had already witnessed animals breeding and the birthing process. It was a fairly easy transition from animals to human behavior with the right modifications, of course. I could not imagine exactly what her reactions would be when she did have her first period, but I prayed daily, asking God to please let it be at home and not at school.

The entire 'developing body' scenario was a pain, for her and me. She needed to wear a bra but her sensory issues played havoc with that idea and she did not want to. It bothered her, it felt funny, it itched, it pinched, she couldn't hook it by herself, etc. She started with a sports bra that had no hooks, but soon had to have more support. I bought one with a front closure so she could see the hooks. She still chafed at the idea of having to mess with it.

She had cramps prior to having her first period. She didn't like that aspect of it at all. Even though her pain tolerance is high, she still complained about the cramps. Then the pads…oh my goodness. If the bra bothered her, it was infinitesimal compared to the sensory issues of pads.

"What if it falls out of my underwear?"

"What if people can see a big bulge in my pants?"

"What if it gets full and blood runs down my leg?"

"It feels funny."

I talked her into trying the pads with the sticky strip on the back to assuage her fears of falling out. She didn't like them. She wanted the ones with wings. Oh, the power of advertising. We purchased the pads with wings. We probably used an entire box, practicing. Putting a pad in her underwear and wrapping those wings around the edges to secure it, then taking it off and putting a new one on. It actually takes quite a bit of fine motor skills to accomplish that and Kalisha was definitely lacking in fine motor skills, but with perseverance, she did accomplish it and could handle it by herself.

I seriously considered buying stock in Kotex. Kalisha changed her pad every few hours or every time she went to the bathroom, whether there was any need to or not. I guess I should have been thankful she erred on that side instead of only changing it every 24 hours.

Her periods were erratic even after she had been having them for a few years. Her doctor prescribed birth control pills so she would become regular and be able to anticipate her start date. Eventually, her doctor put her on the 'depo' shot. The official name is Depo-Provera. She got an injection every 3 months and did not have a period at all. Kalisha was ecstatic about that.

I've spent a lot of words talking about menstruation but that is the foundation or jumping off point for any sexual conversations. She understood the male's role in reproduction and she definitely grasped the reason a woman's period was necessary. Did we discuss all the aspects of sex? No. I gave her answers as she asked them. I always used the correct terminology and words, but gave her the slang words, too. The reason for that was simple. Those were probably the words she was going to hear in everyday comments at school, etc. and I wanted her to know what they were. I had learned my lesson about that when she was only 10 years old.

This was our conversation one day as we were traveling:

"Mom, what's a condom?"

"Uhmmm, well, let me tell you. First, where did you hear that word?"

"Sheri said it today at school."

"Really? Okay." I proceeded to give her a rather short but truthful answer. I noticed she was looking perplexed.

"Do you understand?"

"Not really."

"What exactly did Sheri say about condoms?"

"Well, she said her grandma and grandpa lived in one in Florida."

There's only a few letters difference between condom and condominium but there is a world of difference in meaning.

Kalisha wanted to stop taking the shot but she didn't want to have her period. She spoke to her obstetrician-gynecologist about alternative ways to avoid her periods. She has the most wonderful female ob-gyn. She is soft-spoken, gentle, understanding, speaks to Kalisha as she would to any other patient, and Kalisha loves her. That is very important with any health care professional, but with gynecologists, it is especially important for a girl to feel safe and trust them. With that level of trust, the first pelvic exam was a piece of cake for Kalisha instead of being traumatic.

Her doctor gave her information and pamphlets to help her make a decision. We took them all home and read them together. Even though Kalisha thinks she would like to have a baby some day, she did finally decide to have a procedure that would eliminate periods forever. It would also eliminate the possibility of ever having a child. She told me she would adopt a baby when she got married. Great idea.

We went back to her doctor to tell her about the decision and to schedule the procedure. Dr. B. explained again the finality of the decision. She wanted Kalisha to be fully aware of what she was agreeing to. She left the room for a bit as we discussed it some more.

Kalisha said, "I changed my mind. I don't want to do it. I might want to have a baby when I get married."

I was surprised because she had been so certain.

I stated the obvious. "Right now you don't have a man in mind to marry and then it would still be a while before you would be pregnant. You're almost thirty years old, so it could be another 10 years. I don't think you want a baby when you are 40 do you?"

"Well, Sarah in the bible was 100 years old when *she* had a baby."

I didn't have a good comeback for that kind of logic. It was, at this point, her decision. She told Dr. B. she didn't want to do it; she wanted to continue with the injections. Her doctor supported her in that decision. There is only one drawback to the depo shots. They cause her to be hungrier than normal and therefore add to the weight gain problem.

Kalisha continued to receive the shots for another year, but when she became very serious about losing weight, she made the decision to stop them. Dr. B. prescribed birth control pills to keep her on a regular schedule. She was happy about losing weight but definitely not happy about having her periods again. Many times, life is a 'trade-off.'

Legal Guardianship

HINDSIGHT IS A wonderful thing, if you learn from it. AND if it isn't too late to do what you should have done many years before.

When Kalisha was in high school, her teacher of record, Mrs. M., was a wonderful example of a knowledgeable and caring teacher. She was interested in her students' welfare while in her classes *and* after they graduated.

She asked me if I had taken the necessary steps to become Kalisha's legal guardian. I told her I had not done so. She strongly suggested I should. I nodded and said I would research the procedure. It did not seem important enough at the time so I did nothing about it.

When Kalisha was a senior, Mrs. M. asked me again. I lived in a naïve state of ignorance. I asked myself why I should retain an attorney, spend all that money and time for something Kalisha was never going to need, anyway. I would always be there for her and she would never need anything 'legal' so I did not do it.

I will never be able to express how deeply I have regretted that one decision. In the state of Indiana, where we live, a parent has no control, no options or decision-making abilities once the 'child' reaches the age of eighteen. The circumstances may differ in your state of residence, but a quick internet search leads me to believe most states have the same basic rules.

While you, like me, may feel you will never need to be a legal guardian, please take the steps to have it done anyway. There are many situations, not all of them terrible, when you will be happy you did it. It is much better to have it and never need it than to need it and not have it.

If your child receives a government check of any kind, you can be their payee without being the legal guardian but if you want to actually be able to sign things for them, or if you need to make decisions about birth control, medical treatment, waivers or selection of agencies, you need to be their legal guardian. If your child needs treatment of any kind, decides to enlist in the armed services, decides a plethora of body piercings would look good, wants to get married, rent an apartment, join a cult, buy a house or start a business. These are not all bad things and I realize as parents, we need to be encouraging our child's interests, but wouldn't it be better if you had the right to at least make suggestions or even be able to have the ultimate decision, if the activity was harmful?

There were two instances when I wished with all my heart I had been Kalisha's legal guardian. If I had been her legal guardian, I could have pressed charges in both cases. She also would not have been liable for any purchases because she could not legally sign for anything.

I did use my legal paper, after I had it, to have the police remove Kalisha from a harmful situation. That would not have been possible if I had not been her guardian.

I realize you may be thinking your child would never get themselves into dangerous or unhealthy situations as Kalisha did, but can you be absolutely sure of that? No, you can't.

I am aware of a young man living in a group home. He has no legal guardian; he is emancipated. He makes terrible decisions for himself; 10 new tattoos, buying totally unhealthy food and consuming it all at once. He has no authority parameters and no one to give him any consequences.

Is it an easy process? No. Is it expensive? Yes. Is it emotionally difficult? Very.

This is my experience, in my state, from several years ago. I contacted a lawyer who was versed in this field. She explained the entire procedure so there would be no surprises. Due to the fact Kalisha's father and I were divorced, he had to be contacted, fill out forms and give his opinion of my ability to be Kalisha's legal guardian. All 4 of her siblings were sent papers, also, requesting their input. It is a rather lengthy process; you cannot wait until you need the guardianship before you start the proceedings.

Then came the hardest part of all; the day in court. Kalisha was required to be there and answer questions from the judge. I looked at Kalisha, this young woman I had been telling since she was born how she could do anything and accomplish anything. Now I had to tell the judge she wasn't capable of taking care of herself. The words almost wouldn't come out through my tears. But it was necessary.

The financial cost was $1500, at that time. I am sure it is more now, but you cannot afford to *not* do it. I feel so strongly about this because I put it off and had to learn the hard way. I don't want that to happen to anyone else. The piece of paper won't necessarily keep your young adult out of trouble or prevent them from making really bad decisions, but it will afford you a means of recourse.

If you feel, in your heart, that there might, *ever*, be a situation where your child could be talked into something, might be tempted to purchase something big (a vehicle, for instance) might need counseling or medical treatment or guidance in a difficult situation, then please don't hesitate and don't wait too long

Your child's best interests and your peace of mind depend on it.

Boyfriends, Fiancés and Creeps

KALISHA'S CHRONOLOGICAL AGE and her maturity age have never been in sync, so having a boyfriend wasn't on her radar until she was a teenager and all the other girls were talking about their boyfriends and dates.

She likes to tell people her mother is in love with Tim McGraw (country western singer) and wants to marry him. I remind her he has a beautiful wife and family and he's too young for me, but I like him as a singer and I think he is a good man. She laughs and nods. She knows the difference but somewhere in her thinking, she believes liking someone leads to marrying them. There was a period of time when it seemed as though every perverted male in our city wanted to make some sort of contact with Kalisha. I didn't want to make her paranoid, but I always asked, when she came home, if anything 'interesting' happened that day.

There was the man who pulled her onto the elevator with him and tried kissing her when she was a volunteer at the hospital and taking him to his friend's room.

Then there was the man who approached her as she sat on a bench outside the library. He tried to persuade her to go for a walk with him to some distant park.

While she was the only passenger on a connecting city bus that was parked, the driver came back and asked her to expose her breasts. When we reported his behavior, the bus company told us the tape wasn't in the recorder that day. Convenient.

A man pulled his car over to the curb and asked directions as she was walking on the sidewalk, a few doors from home. When she was close enough to tell him she didn't know the street he was asking about, he exposed himself.

I know she did nothing to encourage their behavior, but something about her walk or demeanor made her seem like easy prey or perhaps they thought she wasn't smart enough to tell anyone. For a period of nearly 2 years, I had the Desk Sergeant's number on speed dial on my phone.

I am not insinuating every person is a monster, but as parents of special needs individuals, we have to work even harder at making them aware of the 'bad' people who may certainly seem like good people to them. Kalisha has become much more discerning and is not quite the easy target she once was.

Her first serious love was Jeremy, whom she met when she was 24 years old. He was several years older than her and very shy. Jeremy lived in an apartment building a few miles from our house and because he didn't drive, he rode the city bus to work at our local grocery. He had been a faithful employee for many years. He was one of the good guys.

While he didn't have any close family, he had learned some of the social graces of dating. He bought Kalisha a heart-shaped box of candy for Valentine's Day and a stuffed rabbit for Easter. He invited her to attend church and bible study with him. He participated in our family's Christmas exchange and went with us to Kalisha's sister's house for the evening .

As Kalisha and I were discussing dating and marriage, she told me Jeremy had sex with some other girl, long before they met each other. It was the opportune time to have that discussion. Just as some people mistakenly believe people with autism have no emotions, it is also often mistakenly believed individuals with disabilities have no sexual desires or thoughts. They certainly have all the desires typical people do; but many times can't express those thoughts or needs. Many people with disabilities can and do have relationships and enjoy marriage, if they have information and support.

Jeremy invited Kalisha and me to his apartment to visit. Jeremy liked NASCAR and had an overwhelming collection of model cars. His apartment was filled with them. As a mother, I was looking around, thinking about the space left for any of Kalisha's things if they ever decided to get married. But of course, I was putting the horse before the cart. Kalisha was not ready to be engaged or consider marriage. She thought she was. But really she was in love with the *idea* of getting married, the ring he gave her and having their engagement pictures taken. The truth of the matter was after telling everyone about it, the excitement wore off.

Jeremy would stop by our house on his way home from work. Many times, Kalisha ignored him and continued watching television. He would get tired of being ignored and leave.

Finally, he gave up and told her he didn't want to be engaged any longer. I believe Kalisha was relieved; however, she will still say, occasionally, how much she liked Jeremy and he was a good man. Yes, he was. I often think they probably would have gotten along well.

There were several years of not being interested in having a boyfriend. Upon entering the house one afternoon, Kalisha announced she had a boyfriend named Luke and they had kissed while on the bus. I didn't overreact (Aren't you proud of me?) I simply asked a *few* questions. You know..inquiring minds want to know. How old was he? Where did he live and with whom? Where did he work? Why was she allowing him to kiss her if she just met him? Was he a special needs individual?

She didn't know all the answers, but over the next week, she filled in most of the blanks. He was fifty years old (yikes), he lived with his mother; his father was deceased. He went to the Catholic church, he had 4 older sisters (uh-oh) he worked at a workshop for disabled people, and she believed he had Down Syndrome.

Kalisha desperately wanted me to meet him and she wanted to meet his mother and his sisters. She asked him every day when she could meet his family. He always told her she could meet them sometime but never set a time. She asked every day for his home phone number; he wouldn't give her that either. He didn't own a cell phone. Kalisha knew his address so she just went to WhitePages.com and found his home phone number….and called him, of course. He told everyone on the bus she was his fiancé. She was excited. They made a decision to be engaged but not get married for a year. I told her that was a very mature decision. They could get to know each other and be best friends by the time they got married.

Kalisha could not understand why he didn't do things like a boyfriend is *supposed* to do. He didn't buy her a card or candy or flowers for Valentine's Day, he didn't want to go on a date; even just pizza and a movie. He was happy just holding hands and kissing her when they were on the bus.

After a few months, she was ready to take things into her own hands. She found an engagement ring online at Wal-Mart, for $30. She showed Luke a picture, he liked it and said he could afford it. He also said it was okay for her to order it. She had it sent to his house because the correct way to do things is for the man to propose to the woman, so it needed to be with him.

The day she received the notification the ring had been delivered, she was ecstatic. She got off the bus with him at his house. Shortly thereafter, I heard the front door open and she asked me to come downstairs. Luke, his mother and Kalisha were waiting for me. She had the ring on her finger but not a happy look on her face.

His mother told me Luke had not told her about the ring or being engaged. She said he would never be married and he didn't even know what that meant. Kalisha explained he called her his fiancé, but Luke's mother said he calls everyone that and he likes to hug and kiss people. Her exact words were that he was *not marriage material.*

After they left, I sat with Kalisha while she put the ring back in the box. I held her and tried to explain it was probably for the best. Who wants to hear *that* when their heart is breaking?

We shed a few tears together and talked for a long time. My tears were for her and her wanting so badly to 'be in love' with someone. I never believed it would end in marriage; there were vast differences in these two people, but I understood her excitement. Once again, she was in love with being in love.

As I sat there, I wondered if she would ever find anyone to marry and if she did, was she prepared to be in for the long haul? Kalisha gets bored with new things pretty quickly. She probably isn't going to find a neurotypical person and yet, the majority of the special needs young men she has contact with, are not able to function nearly as well as her.

Kalisha asked, "Mom, you know how you always tell me God knows if I will get married and if I do, who it will be?"

"Yes."

"Well, when do you think God's going to tell me?"

"I don't know, Kalisha, but I hope He sends me a note, too, so I will be prepared."

I'm Not Going In There

ALTHOUGH KALISHA KNOWS her 'labels' and for the most part, accepts them; there have been times when she did not accept other people with special needs. Fear of something or someone we don't understand is very normal, so in that respect, she was reacting normally.

While in high school, she never wanted to sit at the tables with the students from her 'special ed.' classroom. She would carry her tray to the tables where the football players and the cheerleaders were eating. She wanted to be associated with the popular students. It probably goes without saying she was never allowed to sit with them. They certainly didn't want her in *their* circles.

At one time, we were invited to attend an organizational meeting for a group that was interested in pairing special needs individuals with local college students. The goal was for them to be 'friends' and do some social activities together. There were several young people there who were not verbal, other than making sounds. The plan never materialized, but even if it had, Kalisha was not interested in going back for a second meeting.

We were told about a bible study specifically for individuals with special needs. It was at a local church and sounded like a wonderful idea. She attended one time; I could not convince her to return. She told me she already knew the bible story and the craft was too babyish. Probably true.

This attitude was displayed one Sunday morning. She had a boyfriend, a young man named Jeremy. Jeremy lived in an apartment complex and attended a large church across town. A van picked him up and took him there every Sunday morning. He wanted Kalisha to attend with him. He told her there was a Bible Class first and then the service.

I was fine with the whole idea. Unfortunately, we got up a little late and missed the van at his apartment. I consoled her by telling her I would drive her to his church and go in with her to make certain she was in the correct class. So far, so good.

We arrived just in time to see Jeremy getting off the van and walking in the front doors of the church. By the time I parked, he was, of course, nowhere to be seen. I asked the greeter if he could direct us to the Bible Class designated for disabled people. (That's what the church called it). He graciously guided us down several halls until we reached the door to the class. Kalisha took one look inside the room and started backing up. I was encouraging her to enter the room. Jeremy even came to the door and implored her to come in. She continued to back up until her back was against the wall. She looked at me, Jeremy and the greeter, who was still standing there, probably waiting to see how this was going to play out.

"I'm not going in there with all those handicapped people," she said loud enough to wake the dead.

Jeremy went back in the classroom, the greeter had unobtrusively left the area and I was fuming. I grabbed her arm and herded her down the hall and out the front door to the car.

"What the heck are you doing?" I asked. "I just drove 15 miles, speeding all the way, to get you here in time for Bible Class and you decide not to go in?"

"I don't want to be in a room full of *those people*."

"Did it occur to you that *you* are one of *those people*?"

"No."

"Well, you are, whether you like it or not."

I seethed as I drove to now be in time for the service at our church. Somewhere between one side of town and the other, I started laughing and couldn't stop. The look on the gentleman's face when she made her announcement was priceless and I was trying to imagine what he was thinking. The tears were rolling down my cheeks; Kalisha was looking at me as though I were a crazy person; which we know I am, occasionally.

I made an executive decision to skip all church services for the morning. We stopped for breakfast instead and discussed her reasons for not going into that room. She didn't know exactly how to articulate it, but she was afraid and although she realizes she is different too, she really doesn't see herself that way.

Before you judge Kalisha too harshly, or condemn her for being a snob, I do comprehend how she feels. When my friend, who is my age, was invited to go on a bus trip with the church Seniors' Group, she was indignant.

"I like and respect all those people," she told me, "but I'm not ready to go with them on a trip. I don't want to be lumped in with the elderly."

That's sort of the same thing. Kalisha doesn't want to be lumped in with all the special needs individuals, mostly because she doesn't see herself that way and doesn't want others to see her that way, either.

I have never been able to ascertain the criteria she has for choosing friends.

The Need for Friends

FRIENDS; IT'S SUCH an interesting word. We all want some, we all need some, but we don't always make the best choices when choosing them. That is true of the majority of people, not just people with special needs. Many individuals with autism don't need or want someone to interact with them, but Kalisha craves friends and seems drawn to 'needy' people.

Kalisha and I were standing in the lobby of our bank when she was 3 years old. Several yards away from us were 2 young mothers with little girls Kalisha's age. Kalisha immediately went over to them, smiling. They turned away from her, which is a kid thing, but the 2 mothers put their arms around the little girls as if to protect them from Kalisha. Sadly, I knew in my heart it was a foretaste of things to come.

To say Kalisha has friends would be an understatement of immense proportions. She has hundreds of Facebook friends, numerous acquaintances and some who could only be classified as very needy. And still, if you ask her what she wants, she will invariably say, "I just want a friend." She can't specifically articulate what characteristics she is looking for, but I believe I have an idea. I 'interviewed' Kalisha recently for an article I wrote for Sisterhood magazine. I asked about her expectations of a friend and what she found appealing about some of the 'friends' she chose, especially the undesirable ones. Her best explanation was they talked to her like she was a 'normal' person. They discussed things with her, told jokes, asked her to go places with them; specifically, she was *included*.

When I observe her interactions with some of the young ladies at church, I understand what she means. They are kind to her, they answer her questions but they never really include her in the conversation. They never ask *her* any questions or show an interest in *her* life. They might make plans to go to a movie or a ballgame but never ask her to go along. She may ask for their phone number but they will never call *her*. Why? I believe they have a bit of a fear. Does she need help in the restroom? Will she embarrass them by talking too loudly or make some strange comment? Fear of the unknown is debilitating.

There are some people who genuinely interact with Kalisha. One woman picks her up for a soda and a chat, another takes her for a manicure and pedicure. A man and his wife have taken her bike riding and to a ballgame. Another woman listens as Kalisha tells her about her life or asks for advice. My Amish friend, Rose, taught her to make an angel food cake from scratch and patiently helped her every step of the way.

She had a friend her age named Kathryn, who would make a date with Kalisha every 2 weeks. They would go to the mall or out to eat and visit. When Kathryn got married, she asked Kalisha to come to the room where she was getting dressed and they visited before the wedding.

There have been 2 young men, brothers, who are very good friends to Kalisha. They are both good looking, lots of fun and very gracious. The great thing about these young men is this: when they return from college to their parent's house for a party or any get-together, they never make Kalisha feel different from any other guest. They willingly pose for pictures with her, they find her and sit and visit with her.

A wonderful woman who cuts Kalisha's hair has great conversations with her and leaves me out of them. It is fine with me. She needs an identity not attached to me. Her uncle lives in a neighboring state, but when we visit, he and Kalisha have long conversations about various subjects. I love it.

My friend Kathy likes to tease Kalisha and my friend, Patti, will listen when Kalisha calls her. Brian, Kalisha's brother-in-law, is terrific about listening every time she calls him with a 'Mom problem' or a life problem or she needs to ask a football question. Brian even allowed her to drive the boat and golf cart when we were at the lake. Holy Cow!

Brother-in-law Brian, let her drive the boat

We attend a bible study group at my cousin's home. At the Christmas party; UNO is the game we play. I know it is because Kalisha is able to play it (and win) but they are gracious and make it seem as though it is chosen because everyone likes to play UNO. These are the kind of people you want to have surrounding your child. It benefits both parties.

Now for a few tales of the people you don't want to be your child's friends.

Her first very close friend was Natalie, a high school classmate. Natalie had her own problems, but I believe she genuinely liked Kalisha. She went with our church youth group to an amusement park. She told the leader she would take good care of Kalisha and off they went. She convinced her to smoke a cigarette and ride a huge roller coaster. Neither activity was so terrible, but then she used Kalisha's phone to rack up a $200 bill on long distance calls. (This was before unlimited plans.) Natalie moved to another city and the friendship waned. Kalisha was heartbroken.

During a volunteer job at an elementary school, Kalisha worked with 3 women in the cafeteria. They said they wanted to be her friends, but their main goal was to 'fix' her. They complained about her hair, tried to tell her how to brush her teeth; one even took her shopping for a new bra. She wanted these women to be her friends, but when I complained about their behavior, they sent me a 3-page letter listing all the reasons I was a horrible mother.

There were some weird friendships I have detailed in other chapters. As I've written, Kalisha loved riding the city bus. It was somewhat dangerous sometimes, but I could not keep her from riding. Why? I would have had to tie her to a chair every day to keep her at home. More than that, I understood her need for a bit of independence. I could not deny her that one 'normal' action. After I became her legal guardian, I knew I could call the police if she found herself in a bad situation, so with some boundaries in place, I allowed her to ride the bus. It became more than a fascination; it quickly developed into an obsession.

Kalisha's obsession with the city bus

She rode 6 days a week, usually with a driver named Jolene. Jolene quickly learned of Kalisha's neediness in the friend department and took advantage of it every chance she could. She asked Kalisha to buy her Little Debbie treats, sodas, cupcakes. She parked the bus at a shopping center while she went inside a store to shop and told Kalisha to 'watch' the bus. Right. There was a day when I was admitted to the emergency room at a nearby hospital with chest pains. Kalisha was so obsessed with being on this woman's bus, she would not get off to come to the hospital. She called the ER every fifteen minutes to check on me but would not leave Jolene.

This crazy woman never physically harmed Kalisha but I was afraid she would coerce her into robbing a bank or something equally alarming. I let Kalisha handle this by herself as long as I could, but finally, Kalisha and her Behavioral Consultant and me, had a meeting with the supervisor at the bus company. After that, Jolene would not speak to Kalisha, wouldn't stop to pick her up and was terribly mean to her. Kalisha was sad, mad, disappointed and very hurt.

She soon attached herself to another bus person. This one was in her forties, single and owned a houseful of cats. I think she was lonely and needed Kalisha to listen to her woes. Kalisha is definitely drawn to needy people. Kalisha, who detests the smell of cigarette smoke, would sit in Candy's smoke-filled apartment every day for a few hours and visit.

Unfortunately, most of her friends either don't drive or don't own a car. She has one friend who not only owns a car, but is highly intelligent, attends college, dates, has an apartment and a job. Anne is a good friend to Kalisha. When they go to the movies Anne agrees to see the one Kalisha chooses, even if it might not be her choice. When they go shopping or go out to eat, she reminds Kalisha about overspending and helps her count her money. One evening, she took her along to a bar, where she was meeting friends. I knew Kalisha wouldn't drink any alcohol and Anne assured me she wouldn't drink either and she would keep Kalisha safe. I was thrilled she took her. When they returned, Anne said her friends accepted Kalisha as her friend and asked no questions. They all had a good time, laughing, telling stories, and dancing. I asked Kalisha the next day if she enjoyed herself.

She said, "It was all right, but too dark and too crowded and I think some people were drunk."

I wish I could get some sort of clue as to what attracts Kalisha to certain people. I have been trying to figure it out for a long time, but there doesn't seem to be a rational answer. She would classify the typical young girls who are her friends and do 'normal' things with her as good friends but she is perfectly content to see them once in a while and rarely calls them. She attaches herself like a barnacle to a boat to the individuals who have a few problems, seem needy and are definitely not typical. She wants to see them and spend time with them every day. She calls, texts or e-mails them repeatedly during the day and evening. A few of them became upset with her and blocked her calls and texts. Even though she knows that is going to happen, she is in an obsessive frenzy until it does.

I had a serious talk with her about friends. I asked, "Kalisha, I need you to think really hard about this and I want your honest answer. What is it about Jane, Sara, and Kathy that makes you want to see them every day and talk to them twenty times a day?"

She thought for a while and said, "I don't know. Can I think about that and get back to you?" She really doesn't know or is unable to articulate it, if she does.

Your Card Has Been Declined

MAKE CERTAIN YOU know every adult person your child is going to associate with, even to the point of asking intrusive questions or running a background check on the ones you don't know well. That may sound extreme, but unfortunately, there are many people who see a special needs person as an easy target. It took me too long to learn this.

When Kalisha graduated from high school, we moved from a farming community to an apartment complex while we looked for a house. We were friendly to our neighbors, but we didn't really *know* them. Kalisha wanted to make friends in our new environment, but the teens who lived there only wanted to taunt her.

There was, however, a woman named Deb who seemed to take an interest in Kalisha. She was in her forties and living on disability, which allowed her to be home all day. Deb had a ten-year-old son and a cute Chihuahua named Samson.

She would invite Kalisha to sit on her front step to talk and play with Samson. The next step on this slippery slope was to invite Kalisha to come in and have lunch with her and her son every now and then. I would allow it on occasion, although it seemed odd to me that someone of her age would be interested in being friends with Kalisha, who was chronologically eighteen, but mentally, about thirteen.

I would question Kalisha about their conversations and Kalisha, being very honest, always told me. It seemed innocent enough in the beginning. Soon, Kalisha wanted to get a Chihuahua, just like Samson, then she wanted to go with Deb when she went anywhere; grocery, pharmacy, Wal-Mart. I saw an unhealthy attachment growing.

When I would say no to these little escapades, Kalisha would get upset with me and tell me she wished she could live with Deb and her son. She could be his big sister and Deb had promised she would buy a little dog for her. I knew Kalisha was not coming up with these ideas on her own accord and I was also pretty certain I knew where all this was headed.

One afternoon, Kalisha asked me how much her disability check was every month. When I questioned why she wanted to know, she told me Deb had asked her. Then she proceeded to tell me Deb had told her she could come live with her if she would let her be the 'payee' on her check.

I was not Kalisha's legal guardian at the time and because she was eighteen, she probably could have changed the payee. I don't believe the Social Security office would have done that without making a few inquiries, but stranger things have happened.

I cut off all communication between Kalisha and Deb and much to Kalisha's chagrin, I confronted Deb about the situation. Wonder of wonders, she didn't know what I was talking about.

We moved soon after and left Deb behind. That situation made me painfully aware of the fact that Kalisha would probably always be easy prey for some people. Over the years, there have been many others who would inquire about her monthly income or ask her for money. One man said he would marry her if she would sign her check over to him. She didn't even know his name, but to Kalisha, who really wanted someone to ask her to marry him, it was definitely a temptation.

I made arrangements to have her check deposited directly into a checking account with both our names on it. She had a debit card for the account. I kept it in my possession, but trusted her to take it with her when she was going to buy a specific item, but even that didn't stop the vultures.

Kalisha is notoriously inept about handling money and she used to have a very difficult time saying "NO" to anyone. Putting those two traits together can have disastrous results.

She had a friend, Mary, whom she had known for a year. Mary lived with her mother and their house was only a few blocks from ours. Mary was older than Kalisha, and had been in special education classes when she was in school. She couldn't drive either, so they had a lot in common and became good friends.

I have to insert a warning here: Just because you like and trust a person, do not assume that you can trust *their* friends, if you don't know them.

Mary and Kalisha were going to ride the city bus to the mall on a Saturday afternoon. Kalisha asked for her debit card because she wanted to buy a pair of shoes. When I dropped her off at Mary's house, Mary told me her friend, Terri and Terri's husband, Richard, were going to accompany them to the mall.

Foolish me smiled and said, "Okay, have a good time." Famous last words.

I received a phone call from Kalisha many hours later. She asked, "Mom, What does it mean when it says my card has been declined?"

"Declined?" I sputtered. "Did you say declined?" I knew the balance on that card was over four-hundred dollars when she left home and shoes don't cost that much. I nearly had a heart attack.

"What in the world did you buy?" I asked, trying to remain calm.

"I haven't bought anything. But Terri bought a lot of clothes and stuff and now the lady at the cash register says it is declined."

"Kalisha," I said between clenched teeth, "What else has been happening with your debit card?"

"Well, Terri had her nails done and that cost fifty dollars. Then they all wanted to go to the Mexican restaurant to eat lunch and that cost over fifty dollars for all of us and this is the third store where Terri has bought clothes and jewelry and perfume."

I can honestly tell you that I am not a very nice person when I am furious and I was furious. I asked Kalisha to hand the phone to Terri.

"What the hell is the matter with you?" I screamed into the phone. "I want you to return every last thing you bought."

"Well, they won't take some of it back. I'm wearing some of the clothes and I took the tags off of everything," she whined.

"You had better find the tags, and return as much as you can or I am coming out there right now and you will not be happy if I do that, believe me."

I hung up, still trying to wrap my mind around the fact that a stranger could spend over four-hundred dollars of Kalisha's money.

An hour later, Kalisha called me again and told me Terri wasn't feeling good and called the EMS. All four of them were now on their way to the hospital. My first thought was that I had scared her into having a heart attack. My second thought was that I really didn't care if I had.

I decided it was time to face this situation. I jumped into my car and tried to calm down while I drove the ten miles to the hospital. I know many people don't believe in angels being present here on earth, but I do and I know there was one at the admitting desk of the emergency room that day when I came rolling in.

I smiled sweetly and said, "I know all about the HIPPA laws (privacy laws) and that you aren't supposed to give me any information, but I need to talk to the crazy woman the ambulance just brought in here."

She, (the angel God placed at the desk just for me) smiled back and said, "She's right down the hall in examining room #7."

I marched back there and demanded she give me everything she had purchased with Kalisha's card.

Her husband handed me a few things and said the rest of it didn't have the tags anymore.

"I don't care if it has tags or not. I want all of it and she is very lucky those fake fingernails are glued on, or I would rip them off her fingers and return them, too."

He handed me the bags. I snatched them and walked out, past the desk, where the nice angel lady was not sitting anymore. I found Kalisha and Mary and took them home with me.

Was Kalisha concerned about losing all that money? She realized what her 'friends' were doing was wrong, or she wouldn't have told me the whole story, but the money didn't mean much to her. As long as she had enough left in her account to still buy the shoes she wanted, she didn't care about the rest. What she was more concerned about shows in the question she asked on the way home.

"Do you think you made Terri mad, Mom?"

"Probably, Kalisha. Probably."

"Do you think she will still want to be my friend?"

"I don't think so. But that's okay because she is not a friend."

The next day we returned as much as we could. Only half of it was returnable; the perfume had been opened, some things had been worn. That lesson cost Kalisha over two-hundred dollars, but if the scenario had repeated itself in a few weeks, she still wouldn't have been able to say no to someone she thought was a friend.

We discussed the entire incident and why she let someone she *just met* use her debit card. She really didn't know the answer to that, but she knew she just couldn't say no when someone talked her into something for fear of losing their friendship.

Amazon Woman

ONCE UPON A time….there was a woman who seemed drawn to Kalisha. Yes, another one who wanted things from her. And yes, Kalisha met this one on the bus, also. Her name was Tanisha Jones.

She convinced Kalisha she was an undercover cop, sent to Fort Wayne from Chicago. I tried to explain to Kalisha she would not *tell* anyone if she really was an undercover cop because that was what the term 'undercover' meant. Kalisha wasn't buying my explanation; Tanisha told her she was the only one who knew and she shouldn't tell anyone else. Imagine that.

Tanisha had an apartment on the far end of town, about 3 miles from our house. She had no money for a bus pass or food, so she would walk to the Mission for a free lunch every day, in the 90+ degree heat. Even though Kalisha *had* a bus pass, she walked with Tanisha, because she was her friend. This resulted in huge, water-filled blisters on Kalisha's feet and near seizures for her. She would throw up when she reached the Mission due to the heat and the long walk. Still, she continued to do it, nearly every day.

Once Kalisha left for her daily ride on the bus, I was unaware of where she was going or her activities. There was a day when Tanisha did take the bus to a mobile home park on the north end of town. She convinced Kalisha to accompany her because she needed her help with her undercover work. She had Kalisha approach one trailer and knock on the door while she hid out of sight. Supposedly, Tanisha's ex-husband was living there and she wanted to talk to him, but she wanted Kalisha to ask him to come to the door. The woman who answered the door threatened to shoot Kalisha if she didn't leave her property immediately. Obviously, Tanisha knew that would happen and wanted Kalisha to be the one to get shot instead of her.

I flew to Texas to see my daughter Kari and her family, for a week. Kalisha was comfortable staying home by herself, only because her sister and her family lived next door; within shouting distance. If she needed anything while I was gone, she knew where to go. As I look back on this situation, I cannot believe I actually left her home alone. I suppose I was trying to help her with her independence and perhaps I just needed a break.

While I was there, I received a call one evening around 11:00 pm. It was Kalisha.

"Mom, I'm with Tanisha at some bar and I really want to go home."

"Kalisha, I'm 1200 miles away. What do you want me to do? Never mind. Tell me where you are. What is the name of the bar? I will find someone to come get you."

She told me the name of the bar. I called her sister, Kendra, who lived next door to our house. It was now 11:30. Kendra was in her pajamas, but I assured her she didn't have to go in; Kalisha would be waiting in the parking lot. She assured *me* if she had to go in, she was going to find this Tanisha and whip some ass while she was in there.

I probably should tell you that Kendra is not 'husky' in any way, but she is 6' tall and tough. I had every reason to believe she could and would do it.

I waited anxiously by the phone. Finally, Kendra called and said she had Kalisha and she was home. Then she added, " Mom, have you seen Tanisha?"

At that time, I had not. I said, "No. Why?"

"Because she's an Amazon woman, that's why. I'm not sure I could have taken her down, if I had to. She's probably 6'2 and about 200 pounds. She's got arms like tree trunks."

By now, I was so relieved to know Kalisha was safe, I started laughing and couldn't stop. I have been referring to Tanisha as the Amazon Woman ever since.

I wish I could say that was the last we heard of her, but alas, it wasn't. She left town for a while, but she came back. And once again, Kalisha was drawn in like a moth to a flame.

Tanisha rented an apartment and wanted Kalisha to live with her and a few of her male friends. She also wanted to 'adopt' Kalisha (does a Social Security check come to mind here?) and had her convinced it would be a wonderful life. Kalisha was supposed to share the one bedroom with some guy.

By this time, I had become Kalisha's legal guardian and I had the papers to prove it. I called the police, showed them the papers and said I wanted Kalisha picked up and taken to Parkview Behavioral Health. I thought if she was locked up in the mental ward for 72 hours, she might think about her choices. The fact that I didn't have to give the police officer Tanisha's address because she was well known to them and was in their system, was a scary thought.

I drove to Parkview and waited for the police car to get there with Kalisha. She had no idea why they picked her up or why they were taking her to Parkview, but when she walked in and saw me, she started yelling, at the top of her lungs, "I'm not going home with that woman!" "I'm not going home with that woman!"

You probably think I was devastated. I have to tell you I was laughing so hard, partly from relief and partly because she was somewhere safe. We spent most of the night there, but of course, they didn't admit her. You have to be actively slashing your wrists to be admitted, so by 3:30 in the morning, I brought her home.

She slept for a long time. When she awoke, she told me how sorry she was and she was glad I got her out of there because she didn't want to have sex with the guy Tanisha picked out for her.

To say 'God works in mysterious ways' is not just a cliché. It is certainly true, especially in this case. Due to my efforts to have her admitted to a mental health facility, I was contacted by a state agency. They came to the house, did some evaluations and referred us to a company that could provide a Behavioral Consultant.

All things considered, that was the best outcome that could have happened. There was no way her waiver would pay for a Behavioral Consultant unless it was approved by this agency. I have thanked God many times for the young woman who became Kalisha's consultant, confidant and close friend.

She still has the same BC and we both love her. She is amazing. She immediately started working on helping Kalisha realize her need to say, "No." to people and situations that were unhealthy for her. Did she immediately learn that? Heavens, no. She would take 3 steps forward and 2 steps back; sometimes, 4 steps back. It is a gradual learning process. There are still times she can't say "No" but they are rare. She has grown so much.

He, She,...Who?

KALISHA HAS MET a lot of 'characters' on her many bus rides, but some of them stand out for various reasons; rarely are they good reasons.

She returned home one afternoon talking about an individual named Larry, or Linda. She wasn't sure.

I asked, "You're not sure if it is a man or woman or you're not sure of the name?"

"Well," she said, "I think it is a man named Larry, but sometimes he dresses like a girl and then he says his name is Linda."

"Interesting. How do you know this person?"

"He…she…is a friend of Tanisha Jones."

That explained a lot. "Of course, he..she is." I commented under my breath. Loons always find each other, it seems.

Days went by and Kalisha always came home with another story about Tanisha and HeShe, which is what the name had morphed into. It was easier to say than asking which of the 2 personalities was riding the bus that day.

It was a Tuesday afternoon when she came home carrying a bright pink and black cloth cat carrier over her shoulder. It had little vents on the side, zippers and flaps and looked brand new. In fact, upon closer inspection, it had the tags hanging on it. Before I could ask where she had acquired it, I heard the faint 'mew, mew, mew' coming from inside.

"Whose cats are those?" I demanded.

"Well, they belonged to a friend of HeShe, but he couldn't keep them anymore and I said I would take them because they can't just be dumped on the street."

"Take them out to the front porch. They can't be in the house with our dog and cat. You don't know if they are sick or have fleas or what."

One of the kittens

She emptied them out of their pretty pink carrier onto the floor of the enclosed front porch. There were 2 of them; one was a tabby and the other was as black as coal. They were not very old and scared to death.

My mind was moving a million miles a minute. They would need a litter box of some kind, even for one night on the porch. I had no canned cat food or dry kitten food, only adult cat food. I wasn't certain they were old enough to be weaned.

I found a box lid that would suffice for a litter box, providing they even knew what a litter box was for. I softened some bread pieces in warm milk and tried to figure out what to do with these kittens.

My eyes landed on that beautiful cat carrier. I was pretty sure none of the people involved in this little game had the resources to purchase it. "Kalisha, where did HeShe get this carrier?" I asked as sweetly as I could.

"He stole it from Wal-Mart."

When she saw the look on my face, she hastily added, "But I didn't have anything to do with it, Mom."

"Were you with them when they stole it and walked out with it?"

"Yes. But I tried to tell them stealing was wrong. They told me to shut up and walk out like I didn't know anything."

I guess I don't think like a thief, because I'm trying to put the pieces of this puzzle together. "Who had the cats while you were in Wal-Mart stealing the carrier?"

"Oh, HeShe had them in his bookbag. But he couldn't get on the bus with an animal unless it was in a carrier, so he had to steal one and put them in it, so I could bring them home."

"But they aren't going to stay here, Mom. He and Tanisha are going to get them in a couple of days and take them to their apartment."

"Right, Kalisha. They are never going to come and get these 2 cats, I guarantee it. And on top of that, you are an accessory to a crime."

With eyes the size of saucers, she asked, "Will I go to jail?"

I was pretty ticked off at the whole situation by now and since the other 2 derelicts weren't around to yell at, my first impulse was to say, "Yes, I think you probably will."

I didn't say it. I tried to explain the word, accomplice. Even if you don't touch the item, you are still part of the plan by just being there. I could tell it wasn't making much sense to her.

"So, what should I have done?"

"You should have told them you weren't going to be part of their stealing or you could have told the store manager what they were doing."

She considered those options and then quietly said, "But then they wouldn't be my friends anymore."

For Kalisha, at that time in her life, having friends and being included in things, (even illegal things, obviously) was of the utmost importance.

Of course they never came back for the cats and we did find homes for them but I was still stuck with the damned stolen carrier. I simply could not keep it at my house. I toyed with the idea of returning it to Wal-Mart, but I would have to explain the fact that I didn't want any money back, because my daughter stole it. That would probably not go over well.

Finally, I did what any coward would do…I put it in a Goodwill box. I assuaged my conscience by telling myself it went to a good cause.

Once again, if Kalisha had the strength to follow her convictions, she would not have gone with them, but she wanted their friendship and it felt good to be included. They would not have asked an individual who was 'normal' for fear of being caught and they wouldn't have asked a severely retarded person because they didn't know what they might do…. so they took advantage of Kalisha being "not different enough.'

She encountered the HeShe several more times on her bus rides. One of those times, he asked to borrow her I-Pod and earbuds. She, of course, let him use them. He got off the bus at the next stop and never looked back. The only joy in that situation was the fact that he had no charger so his fun only lasted until the battery died. But Kalisha was minus her $200 I-Pod.

She was upset about it as any kid would be, but she wasn't angry about the cost of replacing it only about the fact she didn't have one to listen to her music. Kalisha's phone and I-pod are very near and dear to her heart. Most people would never let someone borrow an item so important to them, but Kalisha's inability to say No often had terrible consequences for her.

"Work?!" said Maynard G. Krebs

IF YOU WERE alive in the sixties and watching television, you probably know the name, Maynard G. Krebs. A beatnik type, he would yell "Work?!" and nearly faint every time anyone suggested employment of any kind.

Kalisha is like that, sort of. She constantly says she wants a job, but she really doesn't want to work. I will tell you about her volunteering and work experiences and the agencies that were involved. These agencies offer valuable services to many families and individuals. At the time we made use of their services, my opinion was they were geared for physical disabilities and severe mental disabilities. They were not prepared for the individuals who were high-functioning. This is one more time when Kalisha and people like her were *not different enough*.

When Kalisha was in high school, she was enrolled in a job placement program that found part-time jobs during school hours. Her first job was working in the cafeteria kitchen. Her supervisor said she did a great job, when she could keep her in the kitchen. Unfortunately, from her work place, she was able to see the students in line. She would leave her work to socialize with kids she knew. Does that surprise you? It didn't surprise me at all.

Later, she worked with a vocational resource specialist who found her a position at the library in our town. This was a paying job and it was during the summer vacation. Her job was to re-scan books and movies when they were returned to the library. This was done on a machine and she learned it very quickly. This job was in the library's basement. After the first few days of training, she was down there by herself for the entire time. You can imagine how well she liked that.

She worked at a preschool for a semester when school was back in session. She loved it. She made sure everything was ready before the children arrived, she read to them, helped with snacks and anything else they needed. She had a job coach with her.

Before school started in the fall, I was given a video describing the job they wanted her to have for the first semester of her junior year. As I watched, I was amused and saddened. Amused at the thought of Kalisha trying this task and sad they didn't know enough about her to realize this wouldn't fly. I don't know if I could have mastered it. She was going to work in the hospital laundry, preparing the surgeon's gowns for the operating room. There were 23 steps to this process; yes, 23. And of the 23, 17 needed very fine motor skills. Needless to say, she could not do it. By not looking for her strengths, they were setting her up for failure.

There are several problems facing Kalisha when looking for a job. She is not the most motivated individual on the planet. She likes to say she has a job, she likes the uniform, (if there is one) and she likes the people. The paycheck is just a bonus. She doesn't want to work full-time and she doesn't want to work early in the morning. Obviously, I should have worked on skills and motivation a long time ago.

After high school, she worked with an agency that provided job coaches. It is a win-win proposition for employers. They get an employee who doesn't need benefits, is paid minimum wage and they don't have to pay anyone to train them. The job coach will do that.

Here's the problem: when you are involved with an agency, you have the privilege of answering 4-5 pages of questions about your child. They want details of strengths, weaknesses, likes, dislikes and a complete history. I truly don't believe anyone ever reads the answers. First, they tried having this kid who doesn't like extreme temperatures; work in the freezer at a grocery. Then they tried McDonald's working the French fryer; even though she's afraid of flames or hot grease.

She liked the McDonald's uniform

This particular job coach was beginning to annoy me. She took her back to McDonald's for another job. So far, so good. Instead of demonstrating what Kalisha was supposed to do, she sat in a booth, filled out paperwork and verbally told Kalisha what she needed to do.

I received a phone call from her.

"Do you know your daughter doesn't know how to mop a floor?" she screamed at me.

"She probably doesn't. We have carpet everywhere. I never taught her how to mop."

In my mind's eye, I am envisioning one of those industrial yellow mop buckets with the mop that has a handle that's 5 feet long.

She continued, "And she is refusing to scrub the urinal."

I said, "Lady, I'm pretty sure she's never even seen a urinal. We don't have one in our bathroom."

This job coach showed up at my door, still yelling at me. I told her I was totally aware of the fact Kalisha was lazy and it was my fault. But I believed her job was to at least demonstrate the tasks to be done. With that, I ushered her out and told her she was not to return.

We moved on to the next agency and another 5 pages of questions. The person in charge of job coaching here had the strangest idea of how to have Kalisha apply for a job. Instead of going into a potential employer and explaining the benefits of hiring one of her clients, she would have Kalisha take her application in and give it to the manager. I knew the minute Kalisha walked out, the application was tossed. They had no idea there would be a job coach involved.

Being a job coach is a thankless job; long hours, low pay and putting up with the client's parents. Because of that, there is a big turnover in this field, so when you have found the perfect match for your child, there's a good chance they will be replaced by someone new.

Kalisha started applying for jobs on her own. She knew the drill. Turn in your application, call back every couple days to check on it. The song and dance from nearly every employer was the same. They needed their employees to be able to multi-task. Kalisha couldn't operate a cash register or make change. I suggested a job being a greeter at Wal-Mart. She loves people. She would know the 'regulars' by name in a few weeks. The excuse there was they need their greeters to be involved with security. I'm not certain what that means exactly because I'm pretty sure some of the greeters I see at Wal-Mart aren't going to chase down a thief.

Doesn't it make sense to work with the things that interest her? She loves books, movies and children. To me, that suggests daycares, book stores, the library, or a store like Barnes and Noble in the video department. It seemed as though I had come full circle. It was like talking to some of the teachers; they knew everything and didn't want suggestions.

I attended a conference on finding employment for individuals with special needs. It was presented by Indiana University's Indiana Research Center for Autism. The main focus of the conference was to advise parents and agencies they needed to work within the framework of the interests of the clients. Those were the exact things I had been talking about.

We have finally found an agency that is compatible with her needs. It is Bethesda Lutheran Communities.* They not only provide help with volunteer jobs, they have social events, like holiday parties and dances, too. This is also where Kalisha takes cooking classes one day a week.

She volunteered at the chidren's zoo and a large warehouse where returned goods were sorted and put into bins. At the present time, she is volunteering one morning each week in a kindergarten class. She enjoys it very much, so far. Kalisha gets bored with things after a period of time and wants to look for something new.

Her Behavioral Consultant and I have given her some goals. In order to apply for a 'real' job, she has to be faithful in her volunteer commitments. She needs to be pleasant, punctual and cooperative while she is at her volunteer job.

In January, the TinCaps (a local minor league baseball team that she loves) are taking applications. She would like to work for them handing out the programs and greeting people as they come through the gates. I think it would be a job made for her. There are no early morning games, they don't play every day, she could wear their uniform shirt and she could be at her favorite venue. Sounds perfect to me. We will be praying about it.

---

* *This is not a Bethesda book nor is it approved or endorsed by Bethesda Lutheran Communities.*

Write That Down

KALISHA WILL BE 30 years old in a few months, but she continues to make maturity 'jumps.'

The events described in this chapter occurred six years ago, in 2007, when she was 24. I still can hardly write the words on paper, but I feel it is necessary for you to know what can happen to your adult child.

Kalisha's maturity growth has never been a consistent thing. Instead it would seem she was going to be stuck in adolescent mode forever and then, seemingly overnight, she would make a leap to the next level.

She jumped to teenage years in her early twenties. She wanted more independence. She wanted to choose her own friends, talked in whispers on the phone, occasionally forgot to tell me where she was going or when she would be home. (She didn't quite grasp I had done all of this before, although I reminded her of that fact quite often.)

She rode the city bus every day. She knew every route number, every driver's name, where each route could take her and the times she would be picked up and dropped off. Because the bus stop is literally half a block from our house, I felt fairly comfortable allowing her to ride. The bus was her one link to independence. That independence combined with her perceived desperate need for friends whom she thought cared about her, nearly cost her her life.

In one of her travels around the city, she met a young woman named Lucy. Kalisha was enthralled with Lucy's tales of being in group homes, cutting herself, and various other things. She was all 'cured' now, Kalisha assured me. She had her own apartment and a boyfriend and *everything.* Kalisha asked her to come home with her so I could meet her. She seemed like a decent person; friendly, articulate and sociable. But….there was something lurking under the surface that made me uneasy.

Kalisha begged to stay overnight at Lucy's apartment. I refused to let her go. Then she switched to asking if Lucy could spend the night at our house. I finally agreed, thinking it was better to have her where I could keep an eye on her. In the morning, as they were leaving to take the bus back to Lucy's apartment, I noticed she had a wheeled suitcase with her. I inquired about it, but Kalisha told me she was loaning her some of her DVDs. I checked Kalisha's room after they left; all the DVDs were missing; over 150 of them.

I immediately tried to call Kalisha but there was no answer. I tried several more times throughout the day. She finally answered and said she was going to live with Lucy and Lucy's boyfriend, Clay, and I shouldn't try to call her again. The voice was Kalisha's but she didn't sound quite right. I didn't panic. I thought she would tire of them soon enough and be back.

I called every few minutes the next day but her phone went directly to voicemail which meant it was either dead or she had it shut off. Now I was beginning to panic. Remember, I was *not* her legal guardian at this time and she was 24 years old; an adult in the eyes of the law. She could go anywhere and do anything she wanted. She had not been abducted and she was not a runaway; she left willingly with people she knew.

I didn't hear from her for 4 days. I jumped every time the phone rang. Finally it was her tearful, shaky voice, "Mom, can I come home?"

Through my own tears, I said, "Of course you can come home, Sweetheart."

"You don't have a grave dug for me?"

"Kalisha, what are you talking about? Of course I don't have a grave dug for you."

"You won't shoot me when you see me?"

"Honey, I would never do that and besides, I don't own a gun. Let me come get you. Where are you?"

"I can't tell you. I don't know where I am now but I'll be home." She hung up and I fell in a heap on the floor and cried and prayed. I had been begging God for days to let her come home.

I was so afraid I would never see her again, but she did come home on the bus several hours later. Those were the most agonizing hours of my life. I hugged her and cried and asked where she had been and why she didn't answer her phone.

"Clay took my phone and he kept the battery with him so even if I did get the phone, I wouldn't have the battery. They wouldn't let me come home. They hit me and took my medicine and glasses and burned me with cigarettes." She showed me the burns and the bruises. I called the police. The officer took pictures and tried to piece together her story.

She was so tired she couldn't stay awake. The policeman said he would have a detective contact us. Kalisha went to her room and slept the rest of the day.

My friend, Patti, came over that evening because I wasn't sure I would be able to hear the entire story without someone with me. Kalisha sat on the floor and started talking. Patti suggested I write everything down so I wouldn't forget anything when I talked to the detective. As Kalisha continued to add stomach-turning details, she would say each time, "Write that down." Then she would laugh. The laughing seemed inappropriate but I believe it was some sort of release for her.

Clay and Lucy had held her prisoner. They forced her to watch porn movies and then they would re-enact them. She was forced to have every kind of sex you can imagine and a lot you could never imagine, all 3 of them together, occasionally. Lucy took pictures of her being raped by Clay and told her if she tried to get away, they would send them to all her friends and relatives and put them on billboards around the city. These 2 perverted people didn't have a dime to their names so the billboards weren't going to happen, but Kalisha didn't know how much it cost to rent a billboard.

They had her do dishes and fold laundry. If she didn't cooperate, they used several threats. They would take all her clothes and she would have to try to get on the bus naked, they would take her pills and watch her have a seizure, they would do even more inhumane sexual things to her, describing them in graphic detail. She had to go everywhere with them. They didn't let her out of their sight. She went with them to Lucy's doctor appointment. While they waited for her, Clay took her into the restroom and raped her on the floor.

I asked, "Could you have gone to the receptionist and asked her to call me?"

"I was afraid to because he said he would kill you if I did."

She continued, telling us how Clay wanted to get her pregnant so he and Lucy could have the baby. They might let Kalisha hold it for a few minutes but that would be all because she was too retarded to take care of a baby.

Lucy didn't like something Kalisha said and reached out and burned her multiple times with her cigarette. When Kalisha screamed, Lucy hit her in the head so hard it knocked her glasses off and across the room. They laughed as Kalisha crawled around looking for them. She really can't see without them.

They bought candy and cigarettes with Kalisha's debit card until it was finally declined when they were trying to buy dye for her hair. They thought if they changed her hair color, no one would recognize her.

That was when they decided to let her go. She had run out of money and was of no further use to them.

That is definitely not the end of this story. A detective came to the house. Kalisha told him the whole story in more graphic detail than I have written here. He took notes and asked questions. He kept asking Kalisha if she tried to get away. Then we went to the police station and she told him the story over again. This went on for weeks, telling and re-telling the details.

In the meantime, I went with Kalisha to get restraining orders against Lucy and Clay. Clay continued to send Kalisha e-mails telling her he loved her.

The detective finally told me he was sorry but there was an Indiana statute which states, in essence, if Kalisha were *more* retarded, they could file charges. However, since her IQ was listed as 3 points above the cutoff number, she should have been able to escape. Once again in her life, she wasn't quite different enough.

I thought I was going to go crazy. I called my friend, the Director of the Indiana Resource Center for Autism from Indiana University. She offered to come to our city and speak to the police, the judge, anyone necessary to explain why Kalisha would have believed their threats and why she would not have tried to escape. I gave her information and number to the detective. She was never called. I contacted every woman's bureau and organization I could find in the phone book and any I was referred to. As soon as I told them the circumstances and about the statute, the answer was always the same; 'Sorry, we can't help you.'

In the midst of this, I received a call from a mental health facility. The doctor asked if I knew a Clay Harrison. I told him I did, unfortunately. He proceeded to tell me that Clay was a patient of his and although the HIPPA (privacy laws) forbid revealing any information, a doctor *can* divulge what he knows if he believes it is a direct and serious threat to someone.

He informed me Clay told him he planned to burn my house to the ground with me and Kalisha in it. Great. Just what I needed to hear. The lunatic hadn't damaged Kalisha enough so now he was going to burn my house down? That was the first time I seriously entertained the thought of buying a gun.

I called and made another police report. He was never arrested. I saw him on the street the next day and it was only by the grace of God I did not run over him.

Kalisha was examined by her doctor. The report stated there was much evidence of sexual assault. She also stated she thought Kalisha testifying in court would be very traumatic for her. Since there was never an arrest, Kalisha didn't have to testify. A part of me was relieved she wouldn't have to because I knew if a defense lawyer badgered her she would say what he wanted her to say. On the other hand, I wanted nothing more than for them to be found guilty.

I could write 3 more pages of the efforts her father, her siblings and I made to get someone to listen and arrest these 2 people. It was of no use. If I had been her legal guardian, I could have filed charges against them on her behalf.

When the young woman, Jaycee Lee Dugard, was found in a backyard in California where she had been held captive for 18 years, Kalisha was very interested in her story. Jaycee wrote a book about her experiences. Kalisha got it from the library and read it. She asked what was the difference between that girl and her? That girl had chances to escape and didn't. I had no answer for her.

Kalisha still asks sometimes, six years later, if they will ever be punished for what they did. Unfortunately, I have to tell her no; at least not on this earth.

She believes they need to have Jesus in their hearts and for a long time, she prayed for them. I always told her she was doing the right thing and God was smiling at her forgiving heart. When I prayed for them it was to ask they rot in hell. I believe it would have been easier to forgive if they had harmed me, but I was having a terrible time forgiving what they did to Kalisha.

I did a lot of praying about it. I did forgive them, because God wants me to and because I refused to let them occupy any tiny little piece of space in my head. They are non-entities to me.

Kalisha did receive counseling after she was diagnosed with PTSD (post-traumatic stress disorder). She seems to have recovered. She is not fearful of men and no longer has nightmares. I believe her fear is isolated to them, not other people she encounters. With God's help we have both moved on and seldom discuss the events of those days.

However, a few weeks ago, we were at our favorite Walgreen's store.

When Kalisha got in the car, she said, "I have to switch my prescriptions somewhere else."

"Why? We've been getting them here forever."

"I just saw Clay and Lucy in there and I don't ever want to come here again."

I don't suppose the fear will ever leave totally.

Walk of Faith

KALISHA'S WALK OF faith started before she could walk; even before she was born. She was prayed over and prayed for, before the moment of conception.

Of course we prayed for her every day in every circumstance, just as we did for our other children. As the problems Kalisha faced became more evident, our prayers became more fervent. I never asked God to take away any of her disabilities; instead I asked for His help in discovering what those problems were and guidance in how to deal with them.

She was baptized when she was a few weeks old. All 4 of her siblings were her godparents and held her at the baptismal font. That day holds a special place in my heart.

Kalisha learned to say her bedtime prayers and ask a blessing before every meal. That is so ingrained in her subconscious, to this day she can't start eating until she asks the blessing.

She is a Prayer Warrior. She will pray for anyone who asks for her prayers and for people she feels need prayers. Regardless of where we are, when she hears a siren, she will immediately pray for the emergency workers and the people they are going to help.

Baptism Day with her 4 siblings

Bible stories, books and Sunday School were an important part of her life. In many ways she still has the uncomplicated faith of a child. She doesn't try to find answers to every theological question. She knows the stories of the bible, she believes they are true and are God's word; what else is there to know?

She is not shy about asking for prayers, either. When she has some difficulty in her life or impending crisis, she will go to her Facebook page and ask for prayers.

Kalisha has never been shy about sharing her faith. Standing in the produce aisle at the grocery, I was having a casual conversation with an acquaintance. Kalisha, age 6, looked up at her and asked, "Do you know who God is?" The woman, rather taken aback, answered, "Yes." Kalisha continued, "Do you know about Jesus?" and "Do you go to church?" The woman smiled and said, "I used to go, but I don't anymore." Matter-of-factly, Kalisha told her, "Well, you should go again." That was the end of her comments but the woman answered, "You're right. I should." I didn't add anything; I decided Kalisha had said all there was to say.

Due to the fact I worked as the Chldren's Ministry Director at a large church, she was immersed in bible stories, songs, poems, curriculum and children's drama. She was very comfortable in the church setting; it was like her second home. Several mornings a week, the staff met in the sanctuary for a short time of prayer. During the period I homeschooled her, she was with me at church and was included in the prayer times. If for some reason, we did not meet on a scheduled morning, Kalisha would find the staff who attended regularly and remind them it was prayer time.

When it was time for confirmation classes, (6th to 8th grade for Lutherans) many concepts were too difficult for her to grasp, but she attended the classes and listened and went on retreats. Before the actual Confirmation Sunday, the pastor spent one-on-one time with Kalisha, asking her questions. When they were done, he said, "She has an amazing grasp of the fundamentals and when I asked why God should allow her into heaven, her answer was definitely correct." Kalisha told him God would welcome her into heaven because she believed Jesus was the Son of God and she knew He died for her and rose again.

Kalisha has a much more forgiving spirit than I do. She doesn't hold a grudge and will accept every apology offered. She also asks for forgiveness. Some times, too much so. We have a running commentary. When she says she is sorry for something and immediately asks for forgiveness, I often ask, "Is that something that needs to be forgiven?" She will think about it for a bit and decide. I want her to understand the difference between being hateful and disobedient and accidentally stepping on my toes. She can say she is sorry for both, but I don't need to forgive her for stepping on my toes. I don't want her to trivialize forgiveness by asking for it twenty times a day.

When someone hurts Kalisha or is unbelievably cruel to her, she always prays they will find Jesus and accept Him into their heart. She is much more mature in that aspect than I am, but I'm working on it. I can forgive people who hurt me, but I have more difficulty when they hurt Kalisha.

We attend a monthly small group bible study with 6-7 other adults. She enjoys this and never wants to miss. She is first to volunteer to read a section from the bible and gives her opinion, asks questions and answers some. Kalisha is such a social being, she needs the group atmosphere to enjoy bible study.

Regardless of Kalisha's words, actions or disabilities, she knows she is a child of God; loved, redeemed and able to ask Him for help in any situation. She prays for her friends and family to know God's love for them and she remembers to thank God for her many blessings. She is very sure of her salvation and has no doubts concerning where she is going when she dies.

Kalisha's faith is much like the rest of her thought processes; black and white. She knows what she believes, she knows she can gain comfort by talking to God and she is certain of His love for her.

We should all have that simple, child-like faith.

Dreams and Fears—Hers and Mine

KALISHA HAS A few fears; some rational, a few irrational. She has overcome some of them the same way most people do, through peer pressure, necessity or wanting something so badly, she is willing to risk anything to reach the goal.

She always declared she would never ride a roller coaster, but while on a trip to a large amusement park, with the church youth group, a friend talked her into it. She survived, but has never been anxious to try it again.

She climbed a lot of stairs at malls, because she was very fearful of using escalators. While we were in Minneapolis with her niece's volleyball team, the entire group went shopping at Mall of America. She decided to try the escalator. We *sandwiched* her between 2 adults; one in front of her and one behind. She did marvelously and continues to use them by herself.

Her first plane ride was a little scary for her, but the noise the plane's toilet made when it flushed scared her beyond belief. She thought she was going to be sucked out of the plane through the toilet. She was 9 years old at the time and has made several long flights since, but has never used the plane restroom again.

Kalisha has been afraid of using the stove or anything hot since she suffered a burn when she was young. She has been attending a cooking class once a week. This has helped to decrease that fear but has not totally eliminated it.

Heights are probably at the top of Kalisha's fear list. She will not go to any upper levels at sporting events or entertainment venues. Not even at her beloved Indianapolis Colts stadium. She was given free tickets to a preseason game. She checked the seat location on the website before traveling that far, but evidently she misread the seating chart. When she and a friend arrived at the stadium, the tickets were for seats in the topmost section. She couldn't force herself to do it. They came back home without seeing the game.

The above-mentioned things are fears many neurotypical people have but they are more paralyzing to her because she can't logically talk herself through them. What Kalisha doesn't fear are some things she should. She has ridden the city bus to every section of the city, much of which is unfamiliar territory to her, often getting off and exploring stores, by herself. She once got off the bus and walked a mile home after dark, just because she wanted to see what it was like to walk in the dark. There have been several times she has flown alone to see her sister in Texas. I insist she takes a non-stop flight. She is certain she could change planes and find her way through the terminal with no trouble but I'm not willing to take that chance. She has never met a stranger and will converse with anyone. This non-fear has caused her some problems in the past.

Her dreams for her life are a little more complicated. She once thought she would like to be an airline attendant. She printed off every bit of information she could find and filled out the application. She never sent it anywhere, after having second thoughts about the job requirements. She talks often about wanting a boyfriend, getting married, having children or adopting them, going to college, living on her own and driving.

Kalisha would be ecstatic if she could drive. When she was 17, I hired a 'driving consultant.' (He's the person you have come and test your elderly parents' driving abilities before you take their keys away.) He brought his tests and driving simulator to our house. Kalisha was so excited, but her joy was short-lived. When she finished the test and questioned him about her performance, he jokingly told her, "You ran over 2 dogs and a mailman."

She summed up all her dreams and broke my heart at the same time, when I asked her, "What's your biggest dream? What would you like to do more than anything else?" She replied, "Be normal."

The subject of her living on her own has been discussed a lot lately. She would like to get an apartment either by herself or with another young woman. Kalisha, her Behavioral Consultant, and I have talked about the pros and cons of moving and the skills she would need to learn first. Kalisha made a list of the things she needs to know before she could live by herself. Many of the things on the list are things I should have taught her long ago: cleaning the litter box, dusting, vacuuming, washing and drying dishes and laundry. I spoiled her and didn't do her any favors by not insisting she learn these skills. I guess I thought I would be around for her forever. She can do some of the tasks but not totally. For instance, I get the vacuum out and plug it in, she vacuums the floor; I empty the vacuum and put it away again. She can sort laundry and put it in the washer and dryer, but she seldom gets it out and puts it away. She will have to know how to do things totally, not just partially.

The goal she has set for herself is to be ready to move out in a year. She is working on learning self-suffiency. She's talking about it more than she is doing anything about it.

My dreams for her are much the same as hers. I want her to be a self-sufficient young woman who can function on her own, with a little help and overseeing. I want her to get a handle on her understanding of money. I would like for her to find some young man she could spend her life with and be happy. I would like for her to have a job she enjoyed.

My fears are for her safety. I don't want people to take advantage of her or hurt her. I don't want her to be lonely. Many of my fears are for me. I enjoy having her here with me. We don't spend every minute of every day together; we have our own interests and friends and activities, but we are still good company for each other. If I had my way, she would never move out, but I have to think about what is best for her. I don't believe she could handle my death and suddenly being on her own, all at the same time. She needs to be comfortable living on her own before that happens.

Do you remember the animal movies you saw or books you read when you were a child? Somewhere toward the end there was always a scene where the owner had to send the animal away, for its own good; even though they were crying and their heart was breaking while doing it. That is how I feel when I envision her moving. Maybe my biggest fear is that I will be the one who is lonely.

What Happens Then?

I COULD USE THIS chapter to talk about trusts and transfers of guardianship and insurance benefits affecting your child's income, but you can make an appointment with a lawyer to get the answers to those questions. I have chosen to tell you how I am preparing Kalisha for the emotional trauma of my death instead of the financial concerns.

When Kalisha was born and for years after, I concentrated on life; hers and mine. The subject of my death and the subsequent fallout for Kalisha was not on my radar. As I aged, I began to realize when I died, she would be alone for the first time in her life.

She does have a father, of course, but he is 6 years older than me, so, barring me having a fatal disease or accident, the chances of him outliving me are pretty slim.

She also has 4 siblings. I have no doubt they would comfort her and take care of her, but they have families of their own. With the exception of a few vacations taken alone, Kalisha has lived with me for nearly 30 years, 365 days a year.

While I pondered these things, I realized Kalisha has a fairly good outlook on the subject of death. When my mother died, Kalisha was 9 years old. I was advised to not take her to the funeral home for the viewing. I, of course ignored that advice. I knew she needed to see her beloved Grandma.

When we arrived, I watched Kalisha walk to the side of the casket, look at her for a long time and then very seriously, ask, "Why does she have her glasses on? She's not going to need them in heaven, y'know."

Quite typically, she was saddened but didn't shed any tears. However, she did ask if Grandma was going to help Jesus hang the stars in the sky every night. I thought that was so sweet, until she continued, "I want that to be *my* job when I die and go to heaven. I don't want Grandma to get my job." I assured her there were enough stars to go around.

When we lived on the farm, Kalisha had first-hand observations of death when animals died. She didn't seem to be adversely affected by it, but when her little dog, Trixie, was hit by a car, she came the closest to being hysterical I had ever seen.

We have had some great conversations about dying and my death, in particular. She delights in telling everyone I want to be cremated and she's going to spread my ashes on a goat farm. I'm good with that.

On one occasion, she told me, "Mom, you know that perfume you always wear? Well, I'm going to buy a couple bottles, so when you die, I can squirt a little in the air and it will remind me of you." That brought tears to my eyes.

When I attended a 4-day writer's conference in Illinois, she was thrilled to see me when I walked in the door. She was smiling from ear-to-ear and gave me a big hug, telling me how much she missed me. Then she became serious and said, "I guess I better get used to you being gone, because when you die, you're not coming back in 4 days." I certainly hope I'm not.

I am nearly always an upbeat person, but occasionally have a down day. Kalisha asked what was wrong on one of those days. I told her, "I'm depressed and dejected and discouraged, disappointed and disheartened. All the 'D' words."

Her response was, "Well, you're not dead and that's a 'D' word." True. Very true

I know if she is still living with me when I die, she will immediately go to the top of the list for an apartment, as long as we stay in Indiana and she has the waiver. I mentioned in another chapter I think my death and suddenly having to move, happening simultaneously, would be too traumatic for her. It would be better if she were accustomed to sharing an apartment with a friend before I die.

Because I know Kalisha likes to have all her information ducks in a row, I wrote a letter to her detailing exactly what would happen on the day I died. I was as precise as I could be: which sister's house she would go to for the first week, who would help her sort through her possessions, how my things would be divided, etc. I assured her she could take her pets with her. I review it with her every year and change anything that no longer applies. It isn't a will; it is simply a letter of reassurance and I think it makes her comfortable.

I have to tell you I worry about dying and leaving Kalisha here. I occasionally have a few nightmares about her being stuck somewhere with no amenities like her computer and her beloved phone or people being terribly mean to her or all her siblings dying before her or the world coming to the place where all people considered inferior are put to death. (I did say these were nightmares and not necessarily rational thoughts.) I know, without a doubt, her siblings would never allow that to happen, but sometimes, in the middle of the night, those dark thoughts sneak into my head and it frightens me.

I often think of an episode of ER that made me aware of the whole 'My Death' subject. If you don't remember, ER was a television series depicting events in the emergency room of a large hospital.

A special needs young woman was admitted because her heart was failing. The hospital refused to put her name on a list of heart recipients due to her mental disabilities. One of the doctors took it upon herself to organize a campaign to reverse the hospital's decision. It was finally reversed and she was a candidate for a new heart. Her mother, who was an older woman, was not happy. The doctors could not understand why and neither could I. Why wouldn't you want your child to have a new heart and a chance at a longer life? Ah, therein lays the problem. The mother tried to explain her daughter would surely outlive her if she was given a new heart. If she didn't receive the heart, she would most likely die before the mother and she would have peace of mind about her own death and not leaving her child to an uncertain fate.

At the time, I thought that was unconscionable, but I have never forgotten that story and as the years pass, I have come to understand that mother's position. I am not hoping Kalisha dies any time soon, but in all honesty, I would be much more peaceful about leaving this world if I knew she was already helping Jesus hang the stars in the sky.

That's when I hand Kalisha's fate and mine, over to the Lord and allow Him, in His wisdom, to take care of the future.

When I told Kalisha I was nearly done writing this book, she asked, "So, are you going to write another one after the next 30 years?" Before I could say a word, she answered her own question. "Never mind. You'll be dead in 30 years." Probably.

Endnotes

Bethesda Lutheran Communities: A human service organization operating in many states within the U.S. serving people with intellectual and developmental disabilities through faith-based programs. *bethesdalutherancommunities.org*

Indiana Resource Center for Autism: An excellent resource of information for anyone regardless if you live in Indiana or another state. A helpful downloadable brochure can be found at this website: http://www.iidc.indiana.edu/index.php?pageId=32

Recommended FB page: P.R.O.W.D.: Parents Raising Offspring With Disabilities

This page allows you to connect with parents from all over the world, either anonymously or by name. You can get opinions, helpful suggestions or just vent your frustrations.

PROWD is an organization that was birthed out of the needs of those involved in caring for children with special needs and disabilities. It is intended to be a "family" who support, network, and assist one another on their journey.

Recommended movies: 'Temple Grandin' and 'Riding the Bus with My Sister'

2 personal blogs about Kalisha and our life experiences:

www.gettingitright-occasionally.blogspot.com FB page: Getting It Right- Occasionally

www.MOMS.fortwayne.com blog title: Not Different Enough

I have not been compensated by any of the companies or service providers mentioned in this book.

Glossary

ASD:	autism spectrum disorder...a group of serious life-long neurodevelopmental disabilities that appear in early childhood...
Asperger Syndrome:	often considered a high functioning form of autism. It can lead to difficulty interacting socially and repeat behaviors
Inclusion:	special education students staying in the regular classroom for the entire school day
Neurotypical:	a term used for individuals not on the autism spectrum
Waiver:	Medicaid waiver for children is not based on parents' finances and allows access to a wide variety of therapies and assistance. Each state has differing requirements and waiting lists
BC:	behavior consultant

CDC:	Centers for Disease Control
DD:	developmentally delayed
HIPPA:	health insurance privacy and portability act
IEP:	individualized education plan
MIMH:	mildly mentally handicapped

Made in the USA
Coppell, TX
27 January 2021